SOCIOPOLITICAL MUSINGS

VOL .V

Dylan Kyle

Version 1.2

Mandala design: Priyanka Bose

ISBN: 9798389039421

This is an early, working edition of a volume of articles – thus it is version .5.

These articles, and others, are also published online, at www.dylankyle.com. The online versions contain links to source references.

Table of Contents

Are We Reaching Peak Music?

Do people remember peak oil? It's the theory that running out of oil was never the problem, but the crunch that happens after you reach a peak in production.

Like once we empty out all the easy wells and output starts declining, if demand remains the same then naturally there would be less and less to go around. Which would cause prices to shoot up, send shockwaves through the economy.

We have always seemed to manage to find new oil, and the real issue seems to be burning it into the atmosphere. But the pattern must hold for a lot of other things, there's talk of peak cobalt, peak helium, or even peak cocoa. So what I'm wondering here is if it could even apply to something like music. Could we eventually start running out of new songs?

Now, music is admittedly a very infinite and immaterial thing. The question of running out of lithium is something very different than running out of blues riffs.

But what our copyright laws do is create an 'artificial scarcity' – we limit access to music so people have to pay for it, and musicians get paid. And when something is scarce, that implies – almost by definition – that you can run out of it.

There are a few different components of music, but I think this is most relevant to melody. Melodies are the often-repeating sequences of notes that make up songs. The guitar bit from the Rolling Stone's 'Satisfaction', the chorus to the Beatles' 'Yellow Submarine', the guitar solo in 'Stairway to Heaven', all of it is melody (I'm going to use a lot of classic rock examples in this article, as I think it's a genre a lot of people are familiar with, and it's good music).

Really all the guitar bits, verses, choruses, and solos are melody. Alongside rhythm and timbre, melody is basically what music is.

Copyright gives people a monopoly on the melodies in their songs. The Beatles (or actually maybe Sony) own the melodies in 'Yellow Submarine', and they have a legal right to control their use. We don't think about it a lot, but owning a copyright actually gives you a right to censor – if someone uses your melody in a song, you have the right to block that song from being played.

In the real world it usually just works out that the offender has to pay a % of their profits. But legally a song can be silenced. These days it could still end up on Pirate Bay, but that's another story.

There are some exceptions to this, one of the biggest being that you don't need permission to record your own version of other people's songs (a 'cover' song). That's because there is something called 'compulsory licensing' for covers, which is exactly what it sounds like – it's compulsory to give a license. Nobody can legally stop you if you want to do your own version of 'Stairway to Heaven', you just basically have to pay about 10 cents per copy you sell.

You can't change a cover around very much – if you want to change the lyrics, for example, you need the copyright owner's permission. Otherwise we would be hearing 'The Rhythm of the Right' and 'Alt-Right Now' at campaign rallies.

Even translations require permission, although you can import songs into different genres – doing bluegrass or lounge or punk versions seem to be fine. It's kind of a funny thing – covers are allowed, but you can be blocked if you want to use the main 'Satisfaction' riff as part of a completely different song, or even just do hip-hop over a 3 second loop of the drum track (a 'sample').

There are obviously a lot of good reasons why our copyright laws work the way they do. I'm assuming you already know the logic by which copyright allows musicians to make money, and artists deserve to be paid. We don't want giant villain-studios stealing the best songs from all the little garage bands and putting out super-processed versions of them across the radio with subtle political messages.

What's fair aside, musicians would probably still make music without copyright. But it probably wouldn't be as good, and the quality of recorded music in particular could be expected to suffer drastically.

And it goes beyond economic motivations. Having a copyright means that what artists create is theirs – they have control over it, where and how it is used, how it is packaged and sold, what different versions are released, everything.

But at the same time copyright is taking something from the intellectual world, and walling it off into the legal entity that is a song. I'm not going to say that these melodies people own are the building blocks of music. But I don't know if each melody is a unique thing that should only exist in the one original song it was first used in. Do musicians invent new melodies, or are they just discovering them?

Melodies do seem to work in a lot of different musical contexts, there's certainly the potential to reuse bits of songs in other songs. To give an example, I remember seeing it in the news when Sam Smith's 2014 song 'Stay With Me' was accused of copying Tom Petty's 1989 hit 'I Won't Back Down' (I have the tape!).

You can listen to the two of them side by side on Youtube, and it's fairly clearly the same melody, so Tom Petty and cowriter Jeff Lynne got 12.5% each of the songwriting royalties. Apparently a lawsuit was never even discussed – maybe Sam Smith didn't think Tom Petty would let it go.

Nonetheless all parties seemed convinced that it hadn't been theft, that Sam Smith had just come up with the same melody on his own. Tom Petty acknowledged this is a common occurrence in the creative process:

> *"All my years of songwriting have shown me these things can happen. Most times you catch it before it gets out the studio door but in this case it got by. Sam's people were very understanding of our*

predicament and we easily came to an agreement."

So well and good, everything worked out in the end. But from the sounds of it, Sam Smith's song never would have existed if they had realized it was a copyright infringement. And it was a successful song, #1 in New Zealand and Canada, up to #2 in the USA.

As of when I originally wrote this article, it was his most successful song. Since then he's gone in some new directions - Unholy scare-the-conservatives stuff being blared down on us from the grammies, wow.

But a large part of the success of 'Stay With Me' must have been that one melody. Otherwise he's getting pretty ripped off paying 25% of royalties. Although at the same time it feels like he innovated and created something new, it wasn't just a cheap knock off. In Sam Smith's song the offending melody is in the chorus, in Tom Petty's it's the verse.

So maybe melodies aren't getting developed. Fifth Harmony's song 'Worth It' opens with a really good Balkan-Middle Eastern style saxophone sample. The sample seems like something you could do a whole song around, but – noting that I don't actually know the full history and ownership of the sample – I believe it's now locked into that one song.

I could complain here about the message of doing a song about being 'worth it', but I think that would be hyper-critical, maybe it's an affirming feminist message, I've got no problem with that. The rest of the song is good, it was a big hit, but me I wouldn't put it on a playlist and rock out to it driving or anything. I like weird stuff like Balkan music.

You could try doing a 10 minute jazz improv cover of it that said 'give it to me I'm worth it' a couple times at the end, but even that would probably run afoul of the law. The melody and lyrics have to be 'substantively' similar, or it's considered a 'derivative' work, and you need permission to release it. Although there do seem to be some instrumental covers surviving on Youtube.

Even just having melodies linked to certain specific lyrics can be problematic. For one it means a particular bit of music is always tied to one specific story. I don't know if the upbeat tempo and lively melody of CCR's "Bad Moon Rising" really corresponds to its apocalyptic lyrics. Maybe it does, maybe it's connected to some weird woo-hoo it's a disaster mood that's good to be in if you're trying to outrun a hurricane.

But if there are songs like 'Baby It's Cold Outside' that have even questionably disagreeable lyrics (arguably it's a little rape-y), it would be nice to be allowed to just go ahead and change them. Historically bards and minstrels and the like would all do their own versions of lyrics.

There's a classic old British Folk song by Cyril Tawney called 'Sally Free and Easy', which he wrote back in 1958. It's been covered a lot, although maybe there's some consensus in folk circles that Davy Graham did one of the better versions of it – he really brought the melody forward. In actual fact, legally Davy

Graham probably should have gotten permission to change it, even if it isn't so different.

The song is about a perhaps overly easy-going woman who is free of the cares of the world, and heedlessly breaks the heart of a soldier off to war. But the English language has changed around the song with the passing years, and I just don't know if my generation has the maturity to get past the fairly obvious double entendre. Assuming Cyril Tawney wasn't in fact having fun with us.

If you did want to change the lyrics, you would need permission from Cyril Tawney's estate, and I believe Davy Graham's as well, if you wanted to use his melody. The one exception to this would be parody – if you specifically wanted to change the lyrics to make fun of it, that would be legal under 'fair use'. Although Weird Al still makes sure to get legal permission before recording his songs.

Not to single anyone out here. All this stuff is happening *every single time* someone writes a new song. Melodies are getting locked away forever in their original expression. Or if not forever, at least until decades down the road when the copyright expires.

And if these melodies are in fact finite, then I would assume we could start eventually running out of them. Or better reach a peak, where we are still writing new songs, but just not as many good ones as before, while we increasingly start looking back to the classics of yesteryear.

It could well be that whole genres have been denied their later generations. Jazz for one must really be generating a lot of copyrights. A pop or rock song might be based on maybe 5 melodies, while Jazz is laying down 20 melodies a minute.

Maybe this is a polemic thing to say, but I feel like Jazz is very much a genre that had a golden age and has since kept shuffling along, still popular and good but never at its former peak. Or if you look at Rock and the Blues, a lot of it is based on the pentatonic minor scale, which is only made up of five notes, compared to 7 or 8 notes for a lot of other types of music. Just mathematically, that's a lot fewer potential combinations.

Historically music has been made by people borrowing melodies from other songs, modifying them, developing them, bringing them into new genres, doing them in their own style. One of the greatest classic rock bands is Led Zeppelin, who were known for their prolific borrowing. But they improved on the melodies they used, they were definitely innovators who also came up with a lot of good stuff. If you listen to their albums, they really have a lot of good songs.

Likewise a lot of genres – from Blues to Irish Folk to Flamenco to Reggae to Klezmer – developed under conditions without much of any copyright law. They all have public domain melodic patterns that are used and reused.

Mozart would have seen copyright extended to sheet music in the UK during his lifetime, but copyright law either didn't exist or wasn't relevant for the classical composers. They regularly borrowed from each other.

All that said, it is certainly the case that there are really a lot of potential melodies out there. Getting into every star in the sky times every drop of sand on the beach kind of stuff, and that's just using the 12 notes of western music. But most arrangements of those 12 notes don't sound good, try hitting random notes on a guitar.

And if we're talking about the ones that sound really good, there are very few – you can record a hit song if you write a new one. Likewise music seems to concentrate around a relatively small number of patterns – non-musicians are often amazed when they discover how many songs are all the same three or four chords.

Melody is a funny thing, isn't it? That there's just these certain combinations of notes that sound really good, that we like much more than other combinations of notes. To really get to the bottom of this question of peak music, perhaps we need to understand what exactly music is.

And that takes us into some murky scientific waters. Delving into the psychology of music, I'm really struck that we just don't understand why exactly we like music, or how exactly it affects us.

Cognitive psychologist Steven Pinker has called music 'auditory cheesecake' – just a pleasant evolutionary by-product without much meaning. Maybe part of it is showing off fitness to potential mates. Darwin suggested that singing might have acted as a protolanguage on the way to developing proper language and speech – that before talking we all just sang to each other, like the birds.

I for one think music is something pretty profound. One way or another it seems to me that music is communicating something. It has been called the 'language of emotion', it's like a key to inspiring certain states of mind, maybe it even teaches psychological patterns.

I use key in a very literal sense there, because it is very much a key, a code. One distinct pattern of jumps between higher and lower pitched notes unlocks an ecstatic psychological state, while another is random dissonant noise, another is Nickelback.

We must be built for music. You don't need to be taught to appreciate music. And it's amazing how easy it is to remember a complex melody – compare memorizing a melody to an equivalent series of random letters with different durations.

Talking all this classic rock, I feel like the quickest way to understand where people's heads were at during the 60s is to listen to the music. Or that you can understand something of a Turkish state of mind by listening to their lute music.

The question of whether music is universal is actually a little controversial. But they do studies playing people music from cultures other than their own, and people tend to be able to tell if a piece is happy or sad. Or guess at its general themes.

We in the west – at least – tend to associate the major scale with happy music, and the minor scale with sad music, but scientifically we can't say why. That's stranger still given that lots of people seem to find listening to sad music makes them happy.

I for one think we can all enjoy Indian Carnatic Music, Latin American Cumbias, Middle Eastern semi-tones, or Georgian Polyphonies. Maybe it can take a few listens to get into stuff you aren't familiar with. I myself listen to all sorts of music from cultures foreign to me, and I feel pretty solid in assuming I'm getting much of the same experience as they do when I listen to it.

At the same time there is also very clearly individual taste. Which in turn varies according to what kind of mood you are in. Music can be both universal and cultural – this would be the case if all music does in fact represent some kind of underlying fundamental primal emotional code, but certain cultures prefer different codes. The cultural and the individual is the part of the universal that you like.

The exception is the norm, but in North America – for one – there are sort of cultural lines between people who listen to hip hop, compared to country, or classic rock, jazz.

Do these people then have different things going on in their head? Do people in the Middle East experience the world differently because of all the augmented seconds in their music, does Reggae's off-beat give its listeners a distinctive character?

There was a lot going on in the 50s and 60s, but I can't help but wonder if some part of the cultural changes stemmed from using more of the pentatonic minor scale with rock music. Faced with the rise of new

genres like jazz or rock there was a lot of pushback –
people were warning against exactly the sorts of things
that did actually seem to end up happening during those
times. No less than Plato warned that *"musical innovation
is full of danger to the State, for when modes of music change, the
fundamental laws of the State always change with them."*

Who really knows. Given that we don't
understand exactly how music affects us, this is all a
little vague. But maybe another example could be
illustrative here. An old favorite of mine is The
Animal's 'The House of the Rising Sun'. I think I'm safe
in saying it's considered one of the great classics of rock,
a song that has held up over time. It's not a good song
for an open mike because someone might do it before
you. Thus – as with any popular song – I would infer
that it some way resonates psychologically.

The lyrics are a classic morality tale, a gambling
addict looking back on a life wasted on sinful living. I
don't think you really have to be a gambling addict to
like the song though. Melody must not correspond to
something as specific as a set of lyrics, I imagine the
music would work with a variety of similar stories.

But maybe it takes you to a psychological place
where that gambler would be, looking back on life. It's
cathartic, transcendent, seeing yourself and your life
from far away, seeing things as they really are, being
awake, it's a little bit spiritual. Maybe I'm reading in a
bit, and music is just a hard thing to describe in words.
But if you like the song then I get the feeling you are
probably getting an idea of what I'm talking about.

Interestingly, the question of who owns the copyright for that recording is a little complicated. The song 'The House of the Rising Sun' isn't actually owned by anybody – it's considered traditional, it's been passed down the generations and nobody even knows who wrote it. Wikipedia says it probably has roots in English folk music. The earliest known recording is from 1933, by Clarence Ashley and Gwen Foster. Woody Guthrie did a version, as did Bob Dylan, there's a few more recent versions.

The Animal's version is melodically distinct, however, so maybe you could get sued if you used the arpeggio guitar riff or sung melodies in a different song. As a traditional song you're free to do a cover of it though (or even reuse the traditional melodies in a different song), and you can legally do a cover of The Animal's version if you sing it the same way and pay them royalties. I believe you'd have to get permission to sample any of the above-mentioned recordings.

That's because stuff from 1933 is still under copyright. In the USA copyrights from 95 years ago are starting to expire now (it is a little more complicated than that, and every country has their own rules, if they tend to be similar). So on January 1, 2021, music published in 1925 entered the public domain – it's no longer copyrighted, you can do whatever you want with it. And most music from after that is still copyrighted.

In many ways copyright laws are a vast experiment, one which we are smack in the middle of. Most of the music people listen to these days is from after 1925 – or if not, was recorded after 1925. So really almost all of modern music is copyrighted, and owned by a small number of big studios.

While for the vast majority of human history copyright laws didn't exist. In the UK copyright was granted for sheet music in 1777, in the USA it was 1831, Wikipedia says Germany's copyright laws weren't enforceable until 1871. We don't even have a lot of examples of what happens when a genre of modern music goes into the public domain.

So really this is all coming from a very speculative place. But I do feel like we are probably missing out on a lot of good music. I imagine there are some intellectual property Anarcho-Libertarians who want to get rid of copyright law altogether.

There has been a project to use an algorithm to pre-copyright every possible melody then put them in the public domain, but I feel like that's on pretty shaky legal ground. Whether you like it or not, I think getting rid of copyright law altogether is pretty unrealistic, and generally we should put an emphasis on realism when choosing our causes.

And being able to make money from writing songs seems to be an important part of creating music. It is only fair, right? Generally we don't want to reduce the number of people being paid for their work, in this world.

Copyrights do tend to end up being owned by big recording studios, but the fact that big recording studios can own copyrights means they are willing to invest in artists. Which maybe isn't optimal, but it's easy to be overly cynical as well.

It does so happen, however, that there is in fact a very small tweak to copyright law that could probably actually fix this overnight. As I mentioned above, you aren't allowed to use melodies from copyrighted songs without permission, but you can legally do your own version of a song, a cover. This is because there is a system of 'compulsory licensing' for cover songs.

So we could just expand compulsory licensing to include the individual melodies that make up songs. And/or samples of recorded music, although that's sort of a separate question. If Sam Smith wants to use Tom Petty's melody, he can just go ahead and do it, all he has to do is pay royalties. The only real difference would be that the royalty rate is fixed, and the existing owner of the copyright loses their right to block the usage of their property.

That probably sounds like a minor detail, but I really don't think we would want to underestimate what a radical effect this would have on music. As it stands getting a license can be prohibitively difficult, there's generally a lot of expensive legal wrangling involved. That the copyright owner has a veto means they have a really strong hand in negotiations, and often it's difficult or impossible just figuring out who owns a copyright. Which is kind of funny in and of itself, if you think about it.

At this point you might be wondering if there's a catch. There's always a catch with these things, or my logic is flawed somewhere, otherwise wouldn't we of changed the law already? Well, the catch here is that this would do exactly what it says it would do. If I wanted to take the melody from whatever hit song and do my own song around it, I could just go ahead and do that, then put it on the radio.

All the great classic melodies would be re-appearing in all sorts of strange new songs, third-rate musicians would be trying to score hits butchering all your favorites, there would be a blooming of thousands of the singing Sweet Home Alabama song. Listening to music could become a constant guessing game, what's that bassline from!

I assume there would be all sorts of complicated issues to resolve and unintended consequences. I don't know how they would calculate the royalty rate – a standard % based on how many seconds of a song a melody was playing for, or how different it is, if it would be higher for melodies from more popular songs. We could at least block songs based on recycled melodies from being used in things like movies or advertisements – that's how licensing works for cover songs now.

Compulsory licensing could benefit existing copyright holders financially. It could go either way – on one hand having a veto means they can probably get much more for each individual license they give. But with a compulsory license, a much higher % of songs would probably be re-using melodies, so a higher % would be paying royalties.

Generally there are always winners and losers with these things. Maybe people would stop listening to old recordings if new songs were being made with their best melodies. But that can happen with the existing system for covers we have now. Scoring a hit with a reused melody would probably also generate interest in the original.

Sitting down and doing the math, it could be that the group who loses out would be future musicians who write original songs. They would have more competition from music that was reusing old melodies, a higher % of total music profits would end up as royalties paid to existing copyright holders.

Just structurally, future musicians aren't as influential – they're still writing songs in their parent's basements, they can't really throw their weight around as a group. And they would probably be combining their new innovations with old melodies, so it might just work out they write better songs and pay royalties.

But again I don't think the biggest issue here would necessarily be economic. Musicians (and record labels) like having a monopoly over their creations, they only want their melodies to be played in their original song-forms. Requests to sample regularly get denied because the copyright owner doesn't like how they would be used – James Brown for example specified that his music was not to be sampled in anything promoting drugs or violence.

We just get bored of music, melodies would be cheapened if they can be used in whatever song. Classical music offers a case study in how public domain music can be overplayed – the New York Times did an article about how nobody wants to play Für Elise in concert halls anymore. Although this does seem to be less of an issue for other public domain music, like various folk traditions or early music.

There's probably an argument that all this is moot, as well. Musicians could be making requests to license individual melodies under the existing legal framework, but I generally don't think that happens very often. Are the Eagles getting a lot of requests to use the melodies from Hotel California in completely different songs?

Usually whenever someone reuses a melody, it's accidental, or perhaps sometimes more 'accidental'. Such as was in fact the case for Hotel California, which is fairly similar to a Jethro Tull song called 'We Used to Know'.

But one way or another, those accidental uses do seem to happen often enough, and the history of music is a story of borrowing and improving. My feeling is that the issue here is a taboo against using other people's melodies.

It's funny how sampling is seen as much more legitimate. Samples are a reference, a piece of musical collage, creating something new with the old. If they still do want you to get a license. But reusing a melody is seen as straight up theft, and sneaky theft at that, like you were hoping you could just say it was 'accidental' if anybody noticed.

So maybe the root issue – if there is a root issue – is a culture of only using melodies once. And maybe that's ok, maybe they are unique expressions, maybe they only need to exist in their original usage. It could be that the nature of melodies is that they are born perfectly formed. Generally changing a few notes in a melody will either create something that doesn't sound as good, or will be something that the original songwriter has already done during the original song. You don't have to change a melody too much for it to be something new – Jethro Tull never sued the Eagles.

Although even then it would be nice to recombine melodies in new songs, or build on top of melodies. How much of the psychological effects of music are single key melodies, and how much of it is the combination of melodies into the different sections of a complete song? Do you get in the 'Hotel California' mood just straight from the fingerpicked chords it opens with, is it the interplay of the chord progression and the sung melody, would it have a different psychological effect with a different chorus?

It's a nuanced point, but I also wonder how unique each melody is. Can you just listen to whatever bluesy rock song and get pumped into a rock mood, or does each individual melody inspire a certain individual specific psycho-emotional state?

Changing the laws to allow compulsory licensing would probably direct us towards a culture that was more friendly to reuse. There might be some pushback to start, but in the end people would be writing good new songs with old melodies, and I assume it would become more acceptable.

Maybe it could even make cross-cultural pollination more acceptable as well. Aside from music made by Afrodescendant people, there seems to be a slight taboo against using melodic patterns from cultures outside your own.

Cultural appropriation is just one side of the coin, there's also cultural monopolization. As it stands whole groups of musical patterns do seem to be strongly associated with particular ethnicities. Just not being able to change lyrics can make it harder to do covers of songs in foreign languages.

Hypothetically we could also have a compulsory licensing system within the existing legal framework. Copyright holders could just go ahead and allow compulsory licensing for their properties. When you copyright something, you can decide how it can be used, the non-profit 'Creative Commons' has a whole set of alternative types of licenses.

There's databases like that for samples, and the existing system for licensing songs on the radio is very similar to compulsory licensing. Radio DJs generally don't have to get permission for each individual song they play.

Even if the ball got rolling for something like that, it would still be an opt-in system, however. So a lot of the best melodies might still not be available. While I generally think opt-in systems are much more feasible and realistic, people do tend not to opt-in.

All-you-can-eat music streaming services like Spotify have really great selection, but they don't have everything. When a band decides not to put their music on Spotify, that means for you the consumer it's like an all-you-can-eat buffet where you have to pay extra for the crab cakes.

Everyone has to subscribe to Spotify because it has so much good stuff, but then they have to buy that one band's music individually, it's something almost parallel to free riding. If, certainly, there can be good reasons why bands are hesitant. The law could say these services have the right to offer any published song if they pay a royalty – that's another version of compulsory licensing.

I feel like there's a risk of us going in a bad direction in general for those things. If you want access to the full buffet of TV and movies, you have to get a subscription to Netflix, HBO, Disney+, Amazon Prime, and even then that doesn't cover everything.

We could have compulsory licensing for news stories, academic journals, any number of things. Canada used to have compulsory licensing for pharmaceutical drugs, for example. Companies could manufacture generic versions of drugs that were still under patent, they just had to pay royalties. Don't necessarily expect the above-mentioned industries to go out and campaign for compulsory licensing, though.

Those are examples of compulsory licensing for end products. Taking it still another direction, how about a legal right to remake and market documentaries with extra scenes added? People could comment on anything they might feel needed clearing up. There could be a whole aisle in the bookstore dedicated to new versions of Harry Potter with different endings, you could download extra levels for all your favorite video games.

Some of that is probably going a little too far. It's certainly veering further and further off topic. The arguments I have been making here are about something very specific, the legal right to reuse melodies from existing songs.

Melody is something unique, it doesn't have a lot of direct parallels. As it stands you can legally write novels about debonair British Secret agents fighting supervillains in ways that you just can't reuse the 'Seven Nation Army' riff.

Maybe this is a realistic enough cause. This is specifically an example of a very small legal change that would have huge implications. All I'm talking about here is BASICALLY some minor adjustments to the existing laws for cover songs. It could be approached in a minimalistic way. Maximum lengths for samples, prohibitions against obscene or commercial uses, high royalty rates.

It could even just be an exemption that automatically grants compulsory license for similar melodies, as a shield that would limit the maximum payout for people like Sam Smith or the Eagles. There's been some abuse of copyright laws lately, parasitical law firms going after anyone with deep pockets, strange legal decisions like the 'Blurred Lines' case where only vaguely copying the 'feel' of a song was enough for a multi-million dollar penalty.

Compulsory licensing is a minor political issue right now, driven mostly by people who want to make sampling cheaper and easier. No less than MTV themselves have an article arguing for compulsory licensing on their webpage.

A 2016 white paper by the Internet Policy Task Force of the US Department of Commerce did briefly look into a compulsory license for samples, although they didn't think stakeholders were particularly enthusiastic. Compulsory licensing for samples is something slightly different than compulsory licensing for melodies, but I think each of them would probably lead to the other.

In the end, we don't know how music would be different if we had a legal system more permissive of melodic re-use. Nor how exactly that in turn would affect humanity's socio-psychological-cultural state. But I don't think I'm going out on a limb by saying things would be radically different. It would be a pretty big thing, to let anybody use anyone's music.

I imagine some of you would have reservations towards these ideas. And these are reservations that I myself share. More than anything else, my purpose here has just been to try to write an interesting and thought-provoking article about music.

But I do confess that the more I look at it, the more I feel like the benefits for creativity would far outweigh the negatives associated with a loss of control. As it stands, you can legally record any melody out there, you just have to do it in its existing song form. To me it's kind of funny to allow that, but not the usage of those melodies in new and different songs.

Either way, given the assumptions above we are probably going to hit peak music at some point. But this would bump it many years into the future. And in the near term I don't think we're going to run out of new songs. There are whole scales of music from around the world that have hardly even entered into Western music.

But maybe it isn't about the absolute quantity of new songs being written, but of our best melodies being locked into certain very specific and unchangeable musical expressions. Had the Eagles been more worried about lawsuits, it's possible that Hotel California might never have existed. Music is something we really like, something that affects us in profound and mysterious ways. We should do everything we can to maximize the amount of good music that is out there.

CONSUMERS OF THE WORLD UNITE!
(Draft Version)

You have nothing to lose but your chain stores. Actually, you can probably keep them. Buy them out and run them ourselves, even. Woe to those who would underestimate the will of the consumer united. ARE YOU A CONSUMER? THEN THIS IS ABOUT YOU!

Some of you will recognize a reference to Karl Marx in the slightly cliché title of this article. That's a subject a lot of people have strong feelings about - so right out the gate I want to start by clearly stating that this is a very pro free-market article. Likewise, it's not about talking to the manager. Nor boycotts, although they are also a great way of consumers uniting.

No, this is about us consumers taking over the whole show. The marketed-to becoming the marketers. A customer-d'état, consumerism as a cause not a social trend, we the shoppers running things.

Consumers are an interest group like any other, aren't we? Like vegetarians, the coal industry, Australian-Americans, any of them. And as a group we are actually very powerful. Perhaps we're one of the most powerful groups in society. There's certainly a lot of us, almost 400 million in North America alone. And in North America we must at least count double.

We don't see our power, because it's so spread out. Each individual consumer is weak (some exceptions!), but as a whole we are mighty. If you look closely, the tell-tale signs of our power are all around us. What's the old adage, the customer is always right? If someone is always right, it's probably because they are powerful, not because of any inherent wisdom.

There's a sociological rule, that you can estimate at who has power in a relationship by looking at the relative interest/disinterest of each party. And witness how advertisers almost literally chase after us, often with the resigned abandon of an amorous adolescent just trying to get his crush to acknowledge his mere existence.

I mean, how does anybody get rich, aside from selling things to customers? Everybody who wants to be rich is dependent on us. There's plenty of exceptions, but a large share of the fortunes out there must have ultimately been made by selling products to a large number of individual consumers.

Take, for example, a company that sells drilling equipment to three billionaire oil firms. They may only have those three customers. But the oil firms are only buying the drill bits because it's part of the process of selling gasoline and plastic and all that to millions of individual end-users.

But we consumers aren't taking advantage of our latent power. The great leviathan of the consumer still sleeps. Perhaps it's because we have it too easy, we've grown lazy, complacent with the economy around us.

If we want some shiny new material good – say a new TV! – we all just kind of assume that other people will organize the whole design and manufacturing processes, set up a network of stores with showrooms, and ship it out across over the oceans to within ten kilometers of our houses. These days you don't even have to leave the house, you can order it online and they deliver it to the door.

Because we could be making TVs ourselves. That's fully feasible – I mean, if it's just you in your basement, certainly, it's a lot of work, where do you even start? But if it's millions of people, everyone can just chip in a couple of bucks, and we hire some designers, buy wiring wholesale, set up a factory to manufacture them.

Maybe it sounds like I'm ranting and raving, but there is precedence for this. In actual fact it's a thing, a rare and curious beast known as a 'consumer owned cooperative'. Businesses can be owned and operated entirely by their customers.

One of the most prominent examples in the USA is the outdoors store REI. Up in Canada we had our own version, MEC, although they recently privatized under unfortunate circumstances. There's grocery stores, retail chains, in Canada we have a federation of cooperative gas stations. The American Football team the Green Bay Packers is owned by its fans. Credit Unions are financial consumer cooperatives – that they are owned by their members is what separates them from banks, if you were wondering.

Standard model is that they want you to buy a membership, say maybe in the $5-$50 range. Buying that makes you an equal owner of the company - nobody else owns the company, it's just all entirely owned by whoever has purchased the $25 membership. Naturally that means they are generally run democratically, with the member-owners voting for the board of directors.

The pros of the market, and their respective cons

But wait, I can sense something, a trembling on my keyboard, some cosmic quantum reverberations through the network as I type. I've been in enough online debates, your criticisms are already echoing in my soul.

We live in the era of hyper-capitalism, where you can buy everything from vegan human flesh to the Queen's Gambit board game, all with the click of a mouse. Ten minutes of your time gets you magic tickets that can be exchanged for any number of tasty foodstuffs that provide an amount of calories a caveperson 10,000 years ago would have had to spend the whole day hunting and foraging for.

Sure, you say, we could be making our own TVs. But do you know how many TVs there are for sale out there right now? The whole *point* of capitalism is that it lets us be lazy and have TVs delivered to our doors. The whole planet is heating up, not so far from a billion people are going hungry, apocalyptic science-fiction scenarios are starting to become an everyday reality, and your big cause is making even more televisions? Have you even seen the stuff on TV these days?

Well, what consumer owned cooperatives do is get around one of the big main key flaws with free market capitalism. Or more capitalism and less free markets - the two terms do often get used interchangeably, if there are actually some pretty key differences between them.

There are advantages and disadvantages to every way of doing things - if you are looking for a perfect system you'll be searching for a long time. So if I'm complaining about a flaw associated with markets, I also want to gush a little about how they do some amazing things.

Markets really are like ecosystems, with evolutionary patterns occurring, the same sorts of things that drove monkeys to morph into humans. There's variation in how businesses are run, and selection of which businesses are successful. Competition gives you the freedom to go elsewhere if you don't like what's on offer, and that forces companies to make better products.

Beyond any survival of the fittest logic, it's a way to have a self-organizing economy. Obviously someone's organizing things, but it's decentralized - even in this era of mega-corporation monopoly capitalism, nobody's really in control. We all just spontaneously seek out the best ways to make money, and in doing so find our most productive roles, creating and maintaining the economy around us. That's the much-maligned invisible hand of the marketplace.

Historically, organizing an economy without markets has proven difficult – it generally ends up with some centralized establishment running things. You pretty much have to suppress markets, or they spring up spontaneously - with cryptocurrencies we're just always going to have money now, even if we did want to get rid of it.

The economy is an immensely huge thing. Interconnected webs of supply chains stretching from extracting hundreds of different materials to massive intellectual property troves, with myriads of specialists contributing on the way, making products to make products to make products. Even just setting prices becomes difficult, if you aren't using supply and demand.

The market values things by balancing how much people are willing to pay and how much effort it takes to produce them (there's some oversimplifications here), that at least sets some kind of real objective value. Otherwise things get complicated really fast when a bunch of bureaucrats try to figure out how much things should cost. Or who should get how much of what, for that matter. It's truly mind boggling, if you sit down and figure out the sheer number of transactions that go into every transaction to make something even as simple as a can of macaroni and cheese.

But all that wonderfulness aside, we do also live in a massively unequal world, slowly destroying the environment around us, with a culture that seems endlessly co-opted by the quest to sell product. A lot of the various *ists* and *isms* through history have felt that we were getting scammed, that there is a certain unfairness resulting from the existent divisions of property in the world.

The ethical questions are complicated, and perhaps ultimately come down to personal value judgements. But there's something there – earlier I referred to it as a flaw, but I don't know if that's exactly right. I don't even want to call it a problem, maybe problematic is better? Problematic is kind of a loaded term these days, it's used more for stuff like including a turban in your Halloween costume.

Maybe it's a commonly occurring sub-optimal outcome? An accumulative feedback loop with a regressive equilibrium? There's different takes on it, but – boiled down to its essence - this recurring issue with capitalism is the fact that you can make money just purely by owning things. Which in turn basically means that you can make money just by having money.

That's actually a little funny, if you think about it, isn't it? You go out and buy shares in a company, and that makes you money. You don't have to design products, stand over the assembly lines, answer phones, none of it. You just get money because you own a part of the company, and they pay you profits.

Or because the company goes up in value – which is something slightly different, although it's still making money just by having money.

Obviously there's more to it than that. There's a lot of risk inherent in any investment, for one. And just the very act of deciding where to invest is work, and a source of value – people put a lot of effort into deciding where to invest their money, and that does in turn channel it into its most productive uses. Well, actually, most profitable uses, but there is a lot of overlap.

But nonetheless, if you sit down and do the math, a part of virtually all company's profits comes solely from owning things. Maybe an example is useful here. Imagine someone who has some money to invest, and decides they want to open a pizzeria. They rent a restaurant, buy a brick oven and ingredients, and get boxes made. Then they do work around the clock getting the business off the ground.

Once they are successful, they can hire and train a really good manager, and then just ignore the business completely. The manager probably gets a good salary, but the owner is making money as well - they can just sit back and collect the profits.

You can say, well, that's because of all the work they spent setting up the business. And that is true. BUT they can then go and sell half the business to someone else on the other side of the world, and then THAT person would be making profits, even if they didn't have any connection with the business whatsoever. That person just had some money to invest in something profitable.

True, that other investor might have made their money by starting a really nice ethical vegetarian restaurant. Maybe they are just diversifying their portfolio. A lot of smaller restaurants might only work under an owner-operator model – otherwise maybe you're better off with the stock market, it's less stress then finding a good manager. It isn't all a scam. But it is making money just by owning things.

So one interpretation of this is that the pizzeria owner is extracting a surplus from their workers. If it was the workers owning the pizzeria, THEY would be the ones that made the profits. Alternatively we - the eaters of pizza - could be making those profits. Or just paying less for pizza.

This is something very fundamental to our economies, just even to the underlying nature of a world with physical things people can own. To give another example, suppose you have two people, Bob and Fred. Bob owns two houses, while Fred doesn't have any. Bob can live in one house, and rent the other one out to Fred. So just because of the distribution of property in the economy, Fred spends the first week of every month making money to pay Bob, while Bob gets the financial equivalent of a free week of Fred's work. Rents these days, maybe it's a couple weeks.

I imagine I'm not telling most of you anything new. Is this new to anybody? GO AND PUT YOUR MONEY IN THE BANK, THEY'LL PAY YOU MONEY JUST FOR HOLDING IT! Or at least they used to, interest rates compared to fees means most people are losing money on their bank balances these days.

Likewise I don't want you to feel too guilty about making money from your investments. If that's what you get from this article, it is most definitely not my intention. Go make yourself some profitable investments, wherever you feel the most confident, as long as it's not doing anything too evil in the world. You can only ever trust the big wide world out there so much, you do have to look out for yourself and your people. Best you have as much of that pure liquid power in your pocket as you can.

Keep in mind there always tends to be inflation, so if you aren't at least getting a few % returns then you are losing money in real terms. As I write this (the post-pandemic year of 2023) there's talk that we are at the end of an era of cheap money, with inflation reappearing and interest rates going up.

But in the past years we've even had negative interest rates - you invest $1000 in a bond and a couple years down the road they pay you back $950. People made a big deal about that, but it was mostly symbolic - if you are getting 1% interest and inflation is 3%, it's already like you are losing money. You don't really make money by having money unless you are getting positive real returns.

The key point I'm getting at with all this is that every single time you buy things, a part of what you pay is going to people just purely because they own things. You buy some ketchup, part of the money the ketchup company makes works out to be purely because they own the tomato squeezing rig, the bottle assembly line, and maybe the property the factory is on.

The people shipping it are getting money because they own the trucks, as are even the people who fix those trucks, because they have a garage. A kid who has his own lawn mower makes more money than the one who needs to borrow yours.

The Transactdential economics of consumer and owner as one

All that economic logic gets turned on its head with consumer-owned cooperatives, however. The company's owners do still technically get the profits from owning the company - that money has to go somewhere. But when customer and owner are one, it can make more sense just to give yourself lower prices.

The company is still making money by selling things, and the people working for the cooperative are getting paid. It's just that beyond the customers, there are no owners who receive profits, and the revenues the company makes can just go to covering its costs (Costco isn't a cooperative, if you were wondering, but it's about as close as you can get while still being a normal private company).

That said, they can and do pay out cash profits to their owners, like any standard business. But if they do, it's often based on how much you spent during any given year, rather than how much of the company you own. So it works out that you get paid the profits you made selling things to yourself.

The price of a product can be seen as a sum of costs. If, for example, you buy a sofa for $500, maybe $50 goes to the designer, $200 to the factory that made it, of which $40 is for wood, $25 for cotton, etc., then there's maybe $80 to ship it, wages for the factory staff, on like that.

And say $50 goes to the owner(s) of the furniture store that sold it to you. Their profits are what is left over after paying all their costs of running the business. But if you the customer are the owner of that store, that $50 gets taken out of the equation, and you only pay $450 for the sofa. From the cooperative perspective, the owner's profits can be seen as just another cost.

$50 on a $500 sale is probably a reasonable guesstimate at what kind of profit margins an imaginary furniture store is going to have. Or maybe that is a little high, retail tends to have lower average profit margins.

It's kind of funny to ask what the 'average' profit margin is, but a NYU study of a few thousand businesses across industries in the US found an average profit margin of 9.84% in January 2022, ranging from -28.56% for 'Hotel/Gaming' to 32.61% for 'Bank (Money Center).' That's for year two of the Covid Coronavirus, as a point of reference, not a great time for Hotel/Gaming.

Every business and industry is different, they have good years and bad years, invest in future growth.

Plus there's often other perks for the owners like being able to use the company car or going on business trip vacations. It can get confusing just because there are different *types* of profit margins that include different things - the 'net profit margin' has all the expenses deducted and is basically what ends up in the business owner's pockets.

If I'm willing to commit to buying a product every month on Amazon, they offer a 15% discount on a bunch of different products. My assumption would be that both Amazon and the product manufacturer must be making profits beyond that 15%.

Likewise there's a pharmacy down the road that offers seniors 20% off on Wednesdays. Fair enough if you want to argue that the pharmacy wouldn't survive if everything was 20% less all the time for everybody - maybe they can offer that discount because either way they have to pay rent, wages for the sales staff, etc. and the discount gets new customers in the door.

But are they anxiously watching the seniors that day hoping they don't buy very much? You would think the store must at least be breaking even, even with a blanket 20% discount.

Who knows, maybe it builds brand loyalty, 'loss leaders' are a thing, maybe the pharmacy *is* losing money that day. 20% is a pretty big discount. I don't want to oversell things. A 5-10% range is probably much more realistic than 20%. There's some razor-thin margins out there these days - Walmart's management would be reading this saying 5%, if only. Just assuming profitability is something in and of itself.

So it is fair to ask if it would really be worth it. There is risk involved in any business venture - those people who are starting businesses for us are the ones that lose out if we don't want their products. While we can hire people to manage cooperatives, we consumers would have to do some work in setting them up, and put our money on the line.

It's debatable how significant 5-10% is. Looking at it from some angles, it's nothing, from others, it's a lot. If you *can* buy all your food at a cooperative grocery store for 10% less, it adds up. That's a real 10%, not like when they bump up the prices then put them on discount, done properly that's 10% less than what you are actually spending on groceries now. If you work the US average of 260 days per year, 10% of that is 26 extra days of paid vacation.

Furthermore, that's just talking about the grocery store being a cooperative. What if the companies that sell it food were cooperatives, as were the shipping companies that carry them goods, and the farms that grow the raw materials?

Taking the profits out of each of those steps in the production process starts to add up, 10% off here, 5% there, another 7%, and again… In the end, I don't have a clue what % of the price you pay for cornflakes is profit derived purely from ownership. But to hazard a guess, I think it's reasonable to say things could be 60-80% of their current prices in a fully cooperativized economy.

What kinds of endings does self-interest provide?

But what am I doing, I'm getting all obsessed with prices. You can't blame me, can you? Living all my life in this extended-mall of a guess-the-price show materialistic clusterfig. It does something to your psyche, all those hours scanning the grocery store aisles for the loss leaders, browsing disembodied item after disembodied item on ecommerce sites, trying to cross-game loyalty point cards.

For starters, lower prices doesn't have to directly mean lower prices. It could instead translate into higher quality goods at the current price. Or if you want to be more abstract, lower prices could also be higher wages, or a more environmentally friendly production process. A lot of cooperatives just give donations to the community - the Canadian Credit Union Association reports that its member credit unions give an average of 5.4% their of pre-tax 'profits' to local community organizations.

But this widely-defined potential for lower prices is just one advantage of cooperative ownership. Another is that they aren't directly motivated by profit. And to be fair, that can be both an advantage and a disadvantage. The whole idea behind Adam Smith-style Neo-classical economics is that the profit motive is what drives complex economies – that's the invisible hand of the marketplace again. We don't get up early to go to work out of the goodness of our hearts, just like investors don't invest purely for the fun of it.

Now, money is certainly a good motivator, but there are also obviously negatives to running an economy on greed. This article is already longer than I wanted it to be, so I won't give any examples - but maybe you can just spontaneously think of some pithy and poignant examples from your own life.

An interesting corollary to organizing the economy around profits is that technically most businesses don't actually exist to directly do what they do. Chevrolet doesn't exist to make cars, Apple doesn't exist to make phones and computers. They exist to *make money* selling you cars, or phones, or computers. Economically, traditional TV exists only to get you to watch ads - making good watchable shows is just incidental to the process. Sort of a funny place to get your news.

Consumer cooperatives do in fact exist just solely to do the thing that they do. Perhaps that's a subtle difference, but it's a very real one. Nobody directly benefits when the company sells more products, the company could sell 1,000 units or 10,000, and it doesn't really make a difference to the owners.

Obviously that is a matter of degree. Everyone wants their company to do well, and they have to sell products to stay in business. A more successful business is going to be able to make cheaper and better products. But as an economic entity they do exist for an entirely different purpose.

I can't help but wonder how things would be different, if, say, 100 odd years ago, everyone who smoked cigarettes had just started cooperatives to get their smokes. Bought land, hired people to farm it, dry the stuff, roll it up, then made deals with distributors, got it into gas stations. There are real, direct mechanisms - like being able to vote for the board of directors - which would cause the company to truly have the consumer's interesting at heart.

It isn't really in smoker's interests to have other people smoke, for example. Well, maybe a little. The more smokers in a society, the more people there are to talk to on a smoke break. And it strengthens the smoker's right movement, makes it less likely it is they are going to ban smoking on restaurant patios. But I doubt a cooperative would be paying scientists to do fake research, or maneuvering their products into the mouths of Hollywood's greatest stars. Who knows, maybe they'd be compulsively pouring money into anti-cancer research.

One of the classic anti-capitalist parables is the lightbulb that burns out early. It's called 'planned obsolesce' - making a product that doesn't last as long as it could, so you can sell more of the product. It's happened in a lot of industries, but we often use lightbulbs as an example, because there was some truly crazy collusion about limiting how long bulbs could burn for. That only happens because companies are making lightbulbs to make money, instead of just making them so we have lightbulbs.

The free market does put pressure on lightbulb companies to make long lasting bulbs – whenever a company is purposefully making a shoddy product, that creates a space for a new company to get rich selling superior goods. But that doesn't always work properly, there's plenty examples of cartels and collusion throughout history.

And even when the great lightbulb conspiracy isn't on, it's questionable how much manufacturers really prioritize making their products long lasting. It's one thing not to purposefully limit product life, something else to dedicate a huge share of their R+D budget to figuring out how to make products that you only have to replace once every 50 years.

That said - and maybe I'm at risk of sounding snide here - this lack of a profit motive can also potentially be one of the biggest flaws with consumer owned cooperatives. If owning a business is how somebody is getting rich, they are really going to put a lot of energy into it.

This goes beyond the 16-hour days and the 3 AM emergencies, it's about having a huge amount of money invested in something. The owners are steward to a company, they tend to watch it like a hawk, always on the lookout for corrupt management, trying to second guess every swing of the market, obsessing over keeping product quality high.

If a company is owned by five million people, however, it's easy for them to get apathetic. A big chunk of them may be saving say $100 a year by having an awesome cooperative exist. But that isn't going to motivate them like an owner who is making $100 per steady customer.

Another important advantage-disadvantage for consumer owned cooperatives is that being owned by a broader community makes it harder from them to act unethically. It's easy for a rich top-hatted capitalist owner-boss to dump chemicals in a river - they just really need a truck and a crony and voila!

But if it's 200,000 customer-owners having a vote, that's a lot harder to do. It's you the customer-owner who is making that decision to pollute, not some abstract company owned by other people that you have absolutely no connection with, aside from buying their product. Two totally different things there. If, certainly, there are situations where a cooperative's VP of Operations or someone can find a way of personally making money by dumping chemicals in the river. This is about minimizing bad behavior.

I'm again at risk of sounding snide with all this, but I don't mean to be. This is something that does go much deeper than misbehaving executives. Unethical behavior isn't always all about getting the owner rich, but staying competitive in the marketplace.

If all the other paint companies are saving money by dumping chemicals, that doesn't mean they are all making excess profits - maybe they are just doing what it takes to survive. So unless people are willing and able to pay a premium for cleanly produced paint, an ethical paint cooperative is going to find itself priced out of the market pretty quickly. You don't want to underestimate how much slavery and environmental destruction is involved in supporting our middle-class lives in the rich world.

The Ballad of MEC

Perhaps some of these problems I've been raising are behind the recent insolvency and privatization of Canada's most iconic consumer owned cooperative, Mountain Equipment Cooperative (MEC). MEC was and is a big outdoors box store, the type of place with everything from mountain climbing gear to tents to kayaks to astronaut camping rations to high-end rain jackets.

They were originally founded in 1971, by some members of the University of British Columbia varsity outdoors club who were tired of having to go to the US to buy mountain climbing gear. Inspired by the cooperative model of Seattle-based Recreation Equipment Incorporated (REI), they sought to create a similar version in Canada. Starting with just a few $5 memberships in capital, they gradually expanded from operating out of a van with a one-page type-printed catalog, into opening their first store, into becoming a major retail chain, with 5.8 million members in their final days.

All those 5.8 million people were equal owners of the company – you could only shop there if you had a membership, which still cost $5. Technically some people did own extra 'patronage shares' that they accumulated from making purchases. But those didn't give you an extra vote or anything, MEC just purchased them back from you when they had excess revenues – it was basically a rebate.

In the 2018-2019 fiscal year, MEC said they had a net worth (all assets minus all liabilities) of $189 million (this is all Canadian dollars here). More specifically, they owned $372 million in assets, while owing $183 million.

So it's worth noting that the $5 membership bought you a share in the company worth about $40 net. Anytime you can get something worth $40 for $5 that's a pretty good deal. Although that wasn't as good as it sounds – you couldn't sell your share, it just meant you could shop there for the rest of your life.

Ever since I was a kid I remember going to MEC, it was a great store full of genuinely cool stuff. Later I bought a giant travelling backpack from them, and it came with a lifetime warranty. So more than ten years later I brought it back with a broken strap, and they offered to give me half off a new one, or fix it for free.

If you've ever tried to have something like a backpack fixed before (in Canada, at least), you know that's pretty difficult – but they did a bang-up job and I got a few more years out of the backpack. MEC also operated a used gear exchange, and gave a lot of their profits to outdoors charities – about $44 million in total.

But over their final years they gradually went downhill. I don't know if it was any one thing – maybe they had excessively branched-off into stuff like dog food and yoga pants, they made some mistakes going into the bicycle industry? Prices in my local Victoria store weren't below the market - if anything they were higher, it's amazing how much you can pay for a jacket these days. They expanded quite a bit – opening a number of new stores – but that also came with a lot of debt.

In the end they reached a point where they could no longer pay their debts, and had to file for creditor protection. There was a lot going on when that happened – for one, it was just six months into 2020, which was the first year of the great Coronavirus lockdown. Which did actually turn out to be a very good time for retail - there was eventually a big shortage of outdoor goods. At that time, however, it just meant they had been closed for months on end and were bleeding cash.

This economic epoch has just been hard for brick-and-mortar retailers in general, with the rise of online competition. Beyond that, MEC stores in Vancouver and Victoria unionized in the fall of 2019. The directors were warning us beforehand that the company was having financial difficulties, and a union would be trouble.

MEC made a surprise announcement on September 14, 2020 that the company would be privatized and sold, to the US based private equity firm Kingswood Capital Management, LP. The company's member-owners were not consulted about the sale, or even informed about it before that date. It just kind of came out of the blue, like 'oh, hey, we're selling your company.'

The board said they had considered consulting with members to see if they could raise money. But they unilaterally decided it would have been impossible for us to raise enough, and the very act of asking members for funds would have had negative impact on the business. They mentioned the effect on groups like suppliers, landlords, or potential lenders or investors.

It's unclear when exactly they started thinking about privatizing and selling the company, but one way or another it was a long time before the sale was announced. Faced with the coronavirus, on March 27th 2020 they formed a special committee, whose job was to recommend 'strategic alternatives' to deal with their debt. A short document about the committee said:

> *"Strategic alternative transactions may include, without limitation, (a) soliciting interests, proposals and offers from potential partners or purchasers with the view to the sale of all or substantially all or any portion of the assets of the Cooperative."*

By June 10th they had initiated a 'Sales and Investment Solicitation Process'. By June 30th they had entered into confidentiality agreements with 39 parties (narrowed down from the 158 they originally contacted - everybody knew but us!) who were interested in purchasing the company, and sent a process letter. An affidavit by then CEO Philippe Arrata mentions that summaries of all non-binding proposals for the first phase of the sales process were to be received by July 28, 2020.

There were some confounding issues that made it more difficult to talk to members - they delayed the annual general meeting from June to December because of the coronavirus, for one. The results of the election for directors was supposed to be announced at that meeting, so we never even got the official election results for the board that decided to sell the company. Those results were never actually released, in fact.

Naturally there was a lot of opposition to all this from us the cooperative's member-owners. A Gofundme raised about $115,000 for legal fees - more than twice their $50,000 goal. Although a Canadian 'Freedom Convoy' protesting coronavirus restrictions apparently raised more than $10 million. Priorities, I guess.

There was a lot of activism to save the company, mostly revolving around a Facebook group called 'SaveMEC'. Which, as an aside, is a bit of a misnomer, given that the new private company is still called 'MEC' - now it's the 'Mountain Equipment *Company*'. The movement was always about keeping MEC as a cooperative - if all we had wanted was the company to stay in business, we would have been happy with the Kingswood deal as it was.

Try as it might it seems there wasn't much we could to - it went straight to British Columbia's Supreme Court, and after some limited hearings the sale was approved by the court on October 2nd of

2020, with Kingswood announcing that they had completed the acquisition on October 30th. That's 18 days from announcing the sale – again, when the company's owners first heard about it - to it being approved by the Supreme Court. Things can move fast with Canadian corporate insolvency law.

So it worked out that the company's owners were never even given the opportunity to pay their company's debt. Generally, when a company is in financial trouble, it's owners should be given the first chance to bail them out, shouldn't they? There's certain things you just assume in life, without even realizing it's an assumption. Like if you go to a hotel and it turns out the doors don't have locks, you're right to complain, even if it doesn't say locks anywhere on the booking page.

They could have sent an email to every member explaining the situation, asking if they wanted to make a small loan to the company. Me and others were volunteering to call members - with autodialers we wouldn't have needed the confidential lists of contact information, that kind of thing is really easy to set up. People don't mind getting a call or an email if it's about a company they own.

As I mentioned above, MEC did have a positive net worth at the moment it sold – just under $200 million on the books. As of February 23, 2020 their financial data said they held assets worth about $389 million. That included everything, with the two biggest sections being 'inventory' at $109 million, and 'property and equipment' at $262 million.

The same financial document said they owed $230 million – again including everything, even stuff like gift cards. The main issue was just that they couldn't make payment on $74 million of a credit facility with lenders led by the Royal Bank of Canada, which was coming due on September 30th of 2020.

It's also worth noting that as of February 2020 members owned $163 million in 'patronage' shares, which was fairly equivalent to money owed to us. They were MEC's 'profits' which we earned making purchases, to be paid off when the company had extra money. Of course that was suspended with the insolvency proceedings - the creditors got paid first and last. The books also had us owning $29 million from the $5 membership payments.

It would have taken MEC's 5.8 million member-owners less than $15 each to loan the company enough to pay off the $74 million credit agreement. So when the board decided that the idea of having the members bail out the company was so ridiculously impossible that they wouldn't even try it, they were very literally saying it is ridiculously impossible for your average Canadian to come up with 15 bucks. And for a loan at that, it wouldn't have been donations.

Obviously not everyone would have contributed, but lots of people would have contributed thousands, so it could average out to $15 really quickly. Some decentralized file-storage system/cryptocurrency called Filecoin raised $200 million in 30 minutes.

SaveMEC spokesman and organizer Kevin Harding estimated that the perhaps 25-40% of the membership who are considered active members could have raised between $13.5 and $21.6 million with a contribution of $10 each. If we had only raised a few million, that could quickly become enough to get other investors willing to lend to the company, if they weren't willing already.

The SaveMEC team did manage to line up a lot of funding. In an affidavit Kevin Harding reported that a group of three investors had stated interest in a $15-20 million loan, there was a party interested in purchasing $90 million worth of real estate, and a credit card company wanted to do some sort of deal. The Cooperators - a big insurance cooperative - and others were also expressing interest in helping. SaveMEC organizer Yuill Herbert said they had $60-$70 million in pledges.

It just wasn't enough cash in hand though, like was being offered by Kingswood - SaveMEC didn't really have a lot of time to get things together. Personally I'm surprised the government didn't just step in, it was a pretty iconic company.

Bailouts are a thing, you can justify a little special treatment when deals go down like that one did. This sets a dangerous legal precedence, any potential investor in Canada now has to worry about a surprise flash sale of their assets with no compensation to them, even if that asset has a positive net worth.

M-E-C or Meh-ck?

This is all a bit of a disaster story. Maybe I'm not selling you on consumer cooperatives. So let me point out that MEC did run a successful business for 50 years. Lots of successful capitalist firms have problems every 50 years, but their owners are given the opportunity to bail them out. REI was founded in 1938, with 168 locations as of the writing of this article, and revenues of US$ $3.12 billion in 2019. Cooperatives are a proven model.

Every way of doing things has its own advantages and disadvantages. So there are tradeoffs, one set of risks for another, you solve one problem and another pops up. But I don't think problems like member apathy or a difficulty in acting unethically are insurmountable obstacles.

I raise these things because they are the biggest issues with the model that I can see. Really, these are just some of the biggest differences, aside from stuff like that cooperatives tend to be pretty similar to traditional capitalistic firms. I think a lot of people just assume REI is a normal rich-person-owned business like the rest of the economy.

Likewise I don't want to paint MEC as some abject failure in its final years. At its lowest point it was still a pretty good store. But the thing about businesses is they can't chug along at 90% - as we all know, not even 100% is good enough anymore, you gotta be clocking in at more than 110% just on the weekends to make it these days. The company has survived privatization - even in the face of what must be some fairly significant boycotting. You don't need any more proof than that to show that the foundations of the business were solid.

If we're looking for a moral to the MEC story – perhaps someone to blame? – I think ultimately we member-owners should look inwardly. I feel like there was a general sentiment among us for a long time that the company was going in the wrong direction. I remember going to MEC fairly often, but rarely buying anything - that's not actually a weird thing for me, as a point of reference, but it's not a good sign.

Me, I was out there, on the grassroots, bellyaching to my friends about how MEC sucks these days. My little stake in the company motivated me that far. But I wasn't really getting involved – I didn't even vote for the board of directors, nothing.

I wasn't the only member who wasn't voting. In 2016, 53,626 people voted for the board of directors, 57,181 in 2017, 29,798 in 2019. In 2015 they had 4.5 million members, which peaked at 5.8 million - so that is roughly a 1% turnout.

REI has had similar numbers, and I've heard some criticisms on the message boards about them having less than optimal elections. But maybe some things become justified when voter turnout is that low – there's a risk of somebody just getting a bunch of friends together and becoming the CEO of a billion-dollar company.

MEC did a couple of things to try and deal with low voter turnout. They started requiring potential candidates for the board have experience with big companies just to get on the ballot. There's some real and justifiable reasons why they would want to do that, but it raised some hackles. Like someone can only run our hippy cooperative if they've run a super-mega box store chain. I'm sure a certain % of the membership would rather avoid people with that background.

They also started recommending candidates during elections - certain candidates had "recommended" written beside their name on the ballots, and appeared first on the list. The recommended candidates did always seem to win – given the levels of involvement you've seen above, it's my impression a lot of people just voted for the recommended candidates without really putting any thought into it. At one point they entered people in a raffle for gift cards if they voted, which you would naturally expect to provide a lot of votes for the recommended candidates.

Recommended candidates were chosen by a 'nominating committee', which always tended to be made up of three MEC directors, and two members-at-large. The members-at-large were just ordinary customer member-owners (although in 2015 they started serving 3-year terms), who received $300 per meeting to attend. But when the directors have 60% of the votes there's always going to be the risk of a circular thing where the board of directors is basically choosing the board of directors.

It's pretty easy to be cynical about all that. But voter turnout was dismal, there was a general lack of engagement. It is somewhat understandable that they might have felt they needed to recommend candidates.

I also don't want to judge us member-owners too harshly. We're busy people, it's fair to ask how much research we can realistically expect people to do. Beyond that, there's a question of whether your average member can even really do the research needed to make an informed vote – you can do a search for the candidates, read their blurbs, but is that really enough?

Maybe the issue was how they recommended candidates, not the concept of recommendations in and of itself. Us in the proportional representation movement are big on 'citizen's assemblies' – where you get a whole bunch of random citizens together to talk about whether we want to have an electoral system that doesn't inevitably push us towards only having two parties. A cooperative could use a 'customer's assembly' to make recommendations.

Instead of just having two of the company's 5.8 million owners recommend candidates, we could get 200 together. Or even more. We can afford more than $600 per meeting, a half-billion-dollar business like MEC could have invested some real money in choosing its board. Those selected could all meet with the different board members, do roundtables on the direction of the company. There could be a whole big customer conference at the same time, we could stream it online, let all the members participate, it could be an event.

We should expect that it might take some extra work to get consumer democracy working properly. Keep in mind that running a company as a real one-customer-one-vote democracy is the exception, not the rule. How many of your favorite companies are democracies?

The market itself is 'democratic', in its own funny sorts of ways. There are a lot of shareholder democracies out there, some of which are very multi-stakeholder. The whole entire economy itself is a dollar democracy – it's one-dollar-one-vote. Every time you buy something, you are in many ways voting for the survival and expansion of that company.

So that's democratic in the more general sense of the word, like saying the printing press was a democratizing technology, or having the CEO leave early had a democratizing effect on the meeting. Which is something. If you think you have more choice of Presidents or Prime Ministers than laundry detergent you either haven't been paying attention or you live in Europe.

We can structure a cooperative in ways that deal with apathy through policies like candidate recommendation, although the best solution for apathy is just for us all to get more involved. A little bit funny recommending candidates anyways – maybe 2016 would have been different if there was a 'recommended' beside Hillary Clinton's name on the ballots.

We should probably all be getting involved more in general, right? If we want to have democratic systems, we need to do the things that make them work. A lot of elections the world over, voter turnout is really low - regularly just up over the 50% mark, even. Falling below 50% means we don't even have a majority chirping in about who they want giving speeches and what promises they want broken.

Beyond that, only a % of those who vote are really engaged – if it's a particularly insightful focus group ultimately determining a vote, in real terms that vote is in many ways random (or worse). People literally spend millions just trying to figure out the best ways of selling BS to people with your particular personality type, worldview, interests, etc. Doing democracy properly means getting involved, spending some time studying politics, having conversations with people on the other side.

Otherwise we could just go back to monarchy, maybe. Talk to one of the royal families out there, see if they want to take the reins again. Tell them we couldn't handle democracy, we messed it up, look they voted for Boaty McBoathair. You guys should probably just take over again.

That's a different subject, of course – there is only so far you can go comparing democratic companies with choosing the government for your country. And I don't want to say apathy is the only problem here either.

What if the economy as a whole *did* start to cooperativize, and everyone was part of 200+ cooperatives? It would be a pretty big ask to get them to vote for every single board of directors, even if there were big awesome customer assemblies to recommend candidates.

Maybe we could have something like political parties, or you only vote for the directors of holding companies than own 20 cooperatives. Or expand proxy voting, you could just give your vote to someone else to manage. Depending on your local legal framework, that does tend to be allowed for company elections.

It is also debatable what % of a company's customers really need to vote. Less than 1% is probably too little, but maybe it doesn't have to be 70%, maybe even just 5-10% could be enough.

1% voting in an election is nothing, but 1% of customers spending significant time with a non-purchase brand interaction like picking out a candidate and voting for them is actually fairly decent. Just having a critical mass of a few thousand people who are regularly engaging with the running of the company is a powerful thing.

Cooperativize, young consumer

I've really been going off about the problems with consumer democracy, but it's again something that does and has worked well. Pretty cool to have companies where we do all vote for the people who run it, no question of that. By some measures, democratic control is the *best* way of running a company.

One of the things I'm doing with this article is focusing in on the ways cooperatives are different from standard capitalist enterprises, and zooming in on those differences looking for flaws. I think it's fairly logical to assume that in those differences will be the reasons why more cooperatives don't exist. And since cooperatives are so similar to 'normal' businesses - regularly getting mistaken for them - there are limited places to look.

So any criticisms I have of consumer democracy stem from my confusion as to why there aren't more cooperatives out there. A lot of these things are perspective - if you think 'normal' businesses are normal, then a cooperative is a cool exotic thing. But personally I think the whole economy should have cooperativized 100 years ago.

These ideas aren't new. I didn't invent this stuff, if you were wondering - you aren't bearing witness to the time some guy figured out the solution to capitalism.

This idea of cooperativizing the whole economy has been referred to as creating a 'cooperative commonwealth'. Which is where the 'Cooperative Commonwealth Federation' got their name. If you know your Canadian history, they were the political party that combined with the Canadian Labour Congress to form the New Democratic Party (NDP) in 1961.

Cooperatives originally arose with the industrial revolution, and there were cooperative-like organizations as early as the 18th century in the UK.

The Welsh industrialist Robert Owen coined the term 'co-operative and economical society' in 1821. No less than John Stuart Mill became a proponent of cooperativization towards the end of his life, and he was a pretty influential thinker (Mill was into proportional representation as well, eh?).

A key starting point is often seen as when the 'Rochdale Society of Equitable Pioneers' founded a cooperative grocery store in 1844. They published a set of principles for cooperatives which include non-discrimination and democratic member control, and have been very influential in the movement.

From there the movement really grew, to varying extents in different parts of the world. WWII was a setback in a lot of places - Germany for example probably had the biggest cooperative movement after the UK, but it was destroyed by the Nazis and pretty much lived on only in name in Eastern Europe after the war. Likewise the post-war period has been an age of hyper-mega capitalism.

The 60s gave the movement some kind of a boost, but overall since then it's arguably been in a bit of a decline. There's been some corruption scandals, cooperatives going out of business or being privatized. And now all this with MEC.

Still lots of cooperatives out there though. Part of this 'lack' of cooperatives is that you just don't hear about them as much.

A third of the GDP in Italy's Emilia Romagna region comes from cooperatives, and it's one of the richest parts of Europe. The Basque Mondragon corporation is a 24 billion euro worker owned cooperative with operations ranging from finance to manufacturing to construction to retail.

Japan - which has seen its cooperative movement flourish after the wars - has 42,000+ cooperatives with 105+ million members. The International Cooperative Alliance estimates there are more than 3 million cooperatives in the world, employing 280 million people across all the different types of cooperatives out there.

But in the movies, it's always banks being robbed, not credit unions. You might have trouble just finding a Hollywood movie that even mentions cooperatives. When I for one think they should be teaching this stuff in Economics 101. An interesting question to ponder is the ratio to which this is an obvious solution compared to the amount it is talked about. CNN had a segment about cooperatives once.

It's good to avoid being too cynical about the world, but I imagine there must be some powerful anti-cooperative interests out there in the world. Given the price advantages I've outlined above, cooperative can't be fun to compete against, can they?

Back in better times MEC used to get in trouble with manufacturers for selling below their suggested prices – companies stopped selling to them, they had to start manufacturing things themselves. Not the first time cooperatives have been cut off from suppliers for being cooperatives.

It's hard just even to know how much anti-cooperative sentiment there is out there. Cooperatives are such an obviously awesome thing, so it's hard to explicitly go against them. Way worse to be caught doing an anti-cooperative operation than an anti-communist operation, for example.

So keep your heads up, one way or another. Crazy big 'ol world out there. Gotta be careful about listening to those granola-eating hippies, you'll get yourself in trouble with the man.

Either way, a bit of foul play isn't necessarily a sign of an anti-cooperative conspiracy – the marketplace is just a cutthroat jungle of a place for everyone. Your competition might lower its prices so low is it losing money any and all times that another company enters their turf.

Of both-handed cash-grabbing and stash-making

All these various issues with cooperatives I've raised above, one of the single biggest challenges can just be getting the funds together in the first place. It takes a lot of capital to start up a business, it can be hard for a rag-tag band of idealistic consumers to get everyone together to raise the necessary money.

If it takes, say, $10 million to start an appliance manufacturing company, that's a lot easier for a rich person with lots of capital. Just sell a couple underperforming assets, talk to another investor friend, and presto! For a cooperative, you have to find 100,000 people who are willing to invest $100, or a million who are willing to invest $10 each. (If someone in the future is reading this and a loaf of bread costs $10 million, $10 is about the cost of a meal at McDonalds in Canada. Does McDonalds still exist?).

Historically, it's been a challenge finding a million people who are willing to invest $10 each. You'd basically need the mainstream media behind cooperatives, to get those kinds of numbers. But we live in the age of crowdfunding now, and the idea of finding a million people who are all willing to chip in 10 bucks is becoming increasingly reasonable. Especially if it was something really cool.

$10 million will get you a pretty good business these days. And if you can raise $10 million cash in hand, there's going to be people willing to lend you money - you can just assume the company would already have a lot of buzz by that point. Doing some napkin-math, a million people chipping in $10 each is .3% of the US population. I bet there's lots of good businesses that at least .3% of the population uses, and cost less than $10 million to start up.

Suppose everyone in the USA and Canada did just contribute a dollar each towards making a cooperative. Or better 10% of the population chipped in $10, or 1% gave $100 each, one person in a thousand $1000, that's all equivalent. As I write this, we've got 370 million people between us.

Or we could include Mexico as well, actually, to make it a round $500 million - they've got a lot of the same stores, it's the contiguous North American Market. 10% of the population contributing 140 pesos each. Or the Schengen zone would be more than 400 million Euros.

We could start a food company one month, a car company the next, make our own phones the month after that, a social media company, I'm thinking we'd have money left over. We could buy out a polluting company, and clean them up – if you just sell your dirty stocks maybe they just get bought up at a discount by someone less scrupulous (Free investing tip - you can get stock at a discount if you go where others fear to tread and invest in unethical companies - less demand for the stock means the price goes down, and they can be undervalued! That could actually be the story of some industries, if they do tend to attract a certain type of investor..)

Maybe some of the ventures fail - who cares, that's business, maybe others grow to become trillion-dollar companies. To me the numbers sound pretty crazy. Double check my math if you want - 500 million people times .10 (10%) equals 50 million people. 50 million people contributing ten dollars each is $500 million.

Whichever way it works out, it's not a lot of money, but at the same time it's a huge amount of money. Charities send out mailers and they're happy if one person in 200 just writes back, let alone makes a little donation. By some measures, getting a few hundred people to contribute $5 to something is difficult. But in terms of absolute raw potential, 10% of the population giving $10 is pretty insignificant, it's nothing.

Keep in mind that this isn't giving money to the poor or saving the whales. It's an investment in a business. Just like any startup, except the angel investors top out at $25 apiece.

Businesses are kind of magical, they are self-sustaining things. The idea with any business is that it will eventually pay for itself. So if you do the accounting over the long term, profitable businesses are free to start up. Better than free, they make money. The perpetual motion machine is apparently impossible, but successful business can just keep growing and producing and doing what they do, just purely supplied from the profits they make selling things.

The traditional fundraising model for consumer cooperatives is selling memberships. Everybody pays say $25, and everyone is an equal $25 owner of the company. MEC managed to do it with $5 memberships, although that was starting in 1971, there was a lot of inflation in the 70s and 80s.

A fixed membership fee for everyone isn't necessarily going to optimize contributions, however. Some people are only going to be into $10, other people would be happy contributing $100. Some people might be willing to contribute thousands, tens of thousands, if they got something back.

That is actually slightly problematic, for a cooperative. We don't want to give any one person any more of a share of the company. If you do that it isn't a cooperative anymore, it's just a normal capitalist enterprise.

Fortunately there's some easy work arounds. People could just loan money to the cooperative. You invest $5000 above and beyond your $20 membership fee, and you get maybe $10,000 back a few years down the road. It could work like any normal loan, noting that you only get paid back if and when the company is successful.

There's actually a huge number of different ways to organize cooperatives, and there can be different classes of members – user members, worker members, supporting members, etc. Each being structured in a different way, with potentially different voting rights, cost of entry, any number of things.

A cooperative wouldn't even have to have members – we could just raise money entirely by letting anyone invest whatever they want in loans to the company. That's nice and simple – eventually the company just pays off all its debts, and ends up owning itself.

Companies can just own themselves. Maybe that sounds like a weird thing, although we take it granted for non-profits and charities – who owns the American Diabetes Association or the Salvation Army? You can have a non-profit to make salad dressing, just like you can have a non-profit to take care of stray dogs.

Obviously someone needs to manage them, so there could be mechanisms for choosing a board - maybe we get a panel of University professors, business leaders, etc. to pick out who runs the company. If you are skeptical of consumer democracy, there's a model for you. Or inversely, they could just give a vote to anyone who made a purchase in the past year, there's lots of different ways of doing it.

This in fact brings us to an entirely different economic model. Instead of the consumers owning a company, it can be owned by a foundation or a trust. Or just be a non-profit organization.

But – depending on how exactly they are organized - consumer-owned and foundation-owned businesses can be almost identical. Having five million people own a company can work out to be pretty similar to having a foundation own it. A lot of the general themes I am focusing on in this article can be very similar for both cooperatives and foundation-owned companies.

The UK-based Guardian newspaper is a good example of this model. It is owned by the Guardian Media Group, which in turn is owned by the Scott Trust. The Scott Trust was created by newspaper owner John Russell Scott in 1936, so as to protect the newspaper's Liberal stance from potential future owners who might lead it astray.

As it stands, a lot of news companies are owned by a very small number of very rich people. So there is always at least the risk of them unconsciously introducing some sort of bias into their reporting. Every ownership model has its own biases, but one would hope there would be less from a non-profit foundation dedicated to preserving journalistic integrity. The Guardian is a pretty good newspaper, as newspapers go.

Another good example is the food brand Newman's Own, which is owned by the Newman's Own Foundation. It was started by actor Paul Newman in 1982 to sell his popular homemade salad dressing, although it's expanded to a lot of different things now - olive oil, dog food, cookies, coffee.

Nobody makes a profit from Newman's Own. The staff do get a salary, but no owner is getting money from owning the company. As it says on the labels, they give 100% of their profits to charity.

As of 2022 they've given over $570 million to thousands of different charities - summer camps for seriously ill children, programs for veterans, or access to safe water. I'm not going to say that money would all be going to private jets and caviar otherwise - it could be building up people's retirement savings, or foreign investors offsetting their local market risk, all the various types of investing there are out there. But it's still a half billion dollars gone towards doing good in the world.

If all that charity isn't selling you on the idea, keep in mind that $570 million could have just been cheaper salad dressing instead. I hope nobody has any regrets, that money must have done a lot of good. But all those times you were eating the cheap brand, it could have been high quality stuff at the same price.

There's actually a lot of foundation owned businesses out there. Bertelsmann, Heineken, Ikea, Robert Bosch, Rolex, the Tata Group, and Carlsberg are all owned by foundations, for example. Those aren't all necessarily 100% non-profit though.

'Industrial Foundations' (or 'enterprise foundations', I've seen them called 'commercial foundations' as well) are fairly common in the Scandinavian countries - in Denmark they control about a quarter of the country's 100 largest companies. In general Europe has a more foundation-friendly legal environment.

Frequently they were created by the founders of large successful companies as to preserve the company after their death. Often there can be a tax-avoidance angle. They can be a way to pay out to heirs without having the heirs own run the company, but often they do give all or a lot of profits to charities.

Research has found them to perform equally well as 'normal' companies, or even a bit better. Many even have self-appointing boards, where it is the directors deciding if and when and by whom they are replaced – I was complaining about that with MEC.

Beyond foundation-owned businesses, there are also some new models opening up here with new technologies. Companies can be built entirely on computer networks, for example, with their data spread out among thousands of individual user's computers, processing financial transactions through a blockchain like with bitcoin.

I'm not even going to start on this stuff - do a search for 'decentralized autonomous organizations' if your interested. It's interesting if and when a non-business entity like the social network Mastodon can steal users from a company like Twitter. That's taking something out of the market, computer networks just taking care of running our social media.

Talking alternative models, it's worth noting there are other types of cooperatives as well. Agricultural cooperatives are actually one of the biggest cooperative sectors. The Associated Press is a cooperative owned by news organizations. Credit Unions are financial cooperatives, which is a variation on the consumer cooperative model.

A company can also be owned by its workers, in a worker-owned cooperative. Worker cooperatives are great, and I could just as easily write an article like this extolling them as well.

Worker coops are motivated by the profit margin, however, with the advantages and disadvantages that brings – the company's profits are basically the worker's wages. They can also be expected to charge the same prices as traditional capitalist firms. Us consumers are still paying extra, it's just going more to the people who actually did the work making our stuff.

A worker owned business is probably easier to organize democratically. For one it's less people, and each individual voter can be expected to be much more engaged. When it's your livelihood, you're going to care about who the CEO is. With all these different models, it's different sets of advantages and disadvantages, some are going to work better for certain businesses.

Edging towards the actually-do

Any number of businesses could work as a cooperative. But it would be good to do something a little different – ignore what I was saying earlier, manufacturing TVs isn't the best place to start. The people with the SaveMEC movement were talking about starting another outdoors store and recreating MEC, but I don't think that's really gotten off the ground.

For the MEC situation specifically, one solution would be bringing REI up to Canada. I don't know what REI thinks about it, but - full disclosure - I am a part owner of the company, and I think it's a good idea. If enough Canadians became members of REI, it could make sense for them to start opening stores up here to serve their members. As it stands they ship to Canada.

Maybe for some people it's an issue that they aren't a Canadian company. But nobody made any sort of a fuss when the iconic Canadian donut chain Tim Horton's was sold to a Brazilian company. There was a movement to save MEC because it was a cooperative - me for one I'm happy with any solution that gets us a cooperative back.

Likewise the economic logic is different for a cooperative as well. It wouldn't be like profits would be flowing from Canada into a foreign colonizing enterprise – hopefully any extra profits would just go into making better products and lowering prices. And if we made up say 20% of their sales, maybe we could get them to move 20% of their operations to Canada.

Who knows, maybe we have some important insights to provide them after all the happenings with MEC.

Newspapers seem like a good sector to make cooperatives. By newspaper, I mean news agency, news site, YouTube channel, it wouldn't even have to have a print version. The world could use another Guardian, it could use a few more Guardians (another UK newspaper, the Morning Star, is reader owned). When all the newspapers are reporting the same thing, it doesn't mean there's a lack of news. On the contrary, I'd take *that* as a sign we need more newspapers.

The newspaper industry has really been hit hard by the move to the digital environment. Pew research found that between 2008 and 2018, advertising revenues decreased by 62%, while newsroom employment dropped by nearly half. News hasn't become any less important during that time, though.

Personally I think we need an all-you-can-eat buffet approach to the news, sort of like Spotify. Right now news is usually sold as subscriptions to single specific papers. But you don't want all the stories from one newspaper, you want all the stories about the stuff you are interested in from all the different newspapers.

Newsify is a pretty ambitious concept though. News pricing is more complicated than music pricing – news subscriptions vary in price quite a bit, but music CDs (remember CDs?) all cost roughly the same. Starting or buying a newspaper is a quick, easy, here-and-now solution.

Jeff Bezos bought the Washington Post for $250 million in 2013, that's half the $500 million I was talking about earlier. And it doesn't have to be that big - if 10,000 people are willing to contribute $50, that is $5 million. That's decent for a small-medium town newspaper, and they in many ways have had it the hardest.

The individual member-owners could vote for the board, and also vote on what editorial directions they wanted it to take. People would get involved with something like a newspaper. Maybe people would even be willing to accept a loss on their investment, just to have it exist.

A decentralized ownership model also makes it easier to have advertising without as much risk of selling out. If our top-hatted capitalist has to talk to 200,000 member-owners, it's a lot harder for them to threaten to pull their ads when the paper runs a story about an oil spill. Makes it pretty much impossible to just slip the owners some cash.

Who knows, maybe they would find a way – never underestimate the ingenuity of greed. But it would be at least an order of magnitude more difficult. Special interests could be reduced to corrupting specific journalists. But then maybe we could even vote out those journalists. Even a nice shiny cooperative can be a little bit cutthroat when it comes to stuff like that.

How about appliances made out of 100% replaceable parts? The dial breaks on your toaster oven? No need to buy a whole new oven, they just ship you out a new dial and it's plug and play. Maybe for complex repairs you have to take it into a service station. With industrial 3D printers and the like, it's easy to have a pretty sophisticated repair shop out on cheap real estate on the edge of town.

Or what about a grocery store with reusable packaging? There are already a sparse few out there - as well as bulk stores - but I'm thinking something a level up. Invest some real money into it, do it properly.

The model could be like a bulk store, but with a 'we-pack model'. There's displays with product lists, maybe you order on a tablet. Then someone fills containers of various sizes - tupperwares of 200, 300, 500, 1000 grams of dog food, cookies by the sleeve, soap by the bottle. Then they are all waiting for you in bags at the cashier when your comes number is up.

The store would obviously have to wash the containers, so we could let people return them dirty. That's convenient. Bulk washing is more efficient.

We would probably have to charge a deposit on the containers, which could be fairly expensive - my guess is we would need to use fairly high-quality containers. But I don't actually think the price matters that much, as long as people are confident they can get their money back returning them. Maybe we subsidize them a little, and accept that we take a loss if people steal them.

There probably are situations where packaging is important, or not as bad as we think. A small increase in food wastage can make a more minimalist package less green on the balance. Containers do have to be reused a certain number of times to be beneficial. Using petrochemicals for plastic is better than burning them into the air.

But we generate a truly megalithic amount of packaging waste every day, it can't really be that hard to implement a system of reusable containers. Even if the developed world used half the packaging we use now, it would still be a huge amount. Personally I think you could say that about a lot of things, actually.

The environment aside, we do spend a decent amount on packaging. Obviously it varies quite a bit by product, but a study from Ohio State University found that 9% of the price you pay for things is packaging. Some of it comes out of owner's profits, but you are basically the one paying for that flashy chip bag.

There's a lot of little inefficiencies like that in our economy. Advertising costs money, for one. They've just figured out that even with the added costs they still sell more. Even stuff like lawyers for soda companies when someone wants to put a tax on sweetened beverages, or all the money that oil companies spend convincing us that climate change isn't real and it isn't a big deal anyways.

These are again on-the-margin things – reusable packaging still costs money, so it is really hard to say how much of that you actually save. But a few % less on your grocery bill does add up, especially if that's on top of another 5-10% for being a cooperative.

No promises though - there probably are situations where using lots of packaging is in fact the cheapest way. Real problem could be that we aren't properly pricing the damage it does to the environment.

Cooperative takeover

Everything I've been talking about so far has revolved around the idea of starting cooperatives from scratch. But there is another path to cooperativization, in turning existing companies into cooperatives. I can't see any fundamental reason why any existing company shouldn't be able to just turn itself into a cooperative or foundation. Just gotta have 51% of the shareholders behind it.

There was a movement to turn Twitter into a user-owned cooperative. The users are generating all the content, the Twitter platform is just the underlying infrastructure. So why not have the users own it? It's sort of gone the other direction now with Elon Musk buying it.

Big famous companies are really worth a lot - and can arguably be over-valued - so they might be hard targets. But their high profile could make it easier as well, if something like that ever really started to get off the ground. Just in general buying established companies is more expensive than starting companies, assuming the companies you start do in fact get off the ground. People start billion-dollar companies in their basement with $500.

But suppose we did want to buy Twitter. Doing some more napkin-calculations, Elon Musk bought Twitter for US $44 billion. So we can value the company at 44 billion - the internet tells me it's only worth $41 billion now, you could probably argue a few different prices, but $44 billion is good for napkin-math.

As of 2022 Twitter had 238 million 'active daily users'. The actual number of users is higher - those are just the people who use it every day. But I'm sure some of them are bots - this is all rough estimations. But going with just the 238 million, it would cost each of them a little less than US $200 each to buy the company.

If you are going to ask everyone to cough up $200 to keep using Twitter, that probably wouldn't happen. But $20 per year for 10 years isn't so bad, or even $10 per year for 20 years.

That wouldn't necessarily have to be out-of-pocket, the company's revenues could go towards it. In 2021 Twitter made revenues of $5.1 billion dollars - that's dropped since it privatized, however, and obviously we wouldn't be able to use all that to buy itself. Revenue is the total of what a company brings in, you gotta subtract all the expenses to get profits.

Here's a wacky strategy for you. We start a foundation, which takes out a loan to buy shares in a company on the stock market. We cough up the money for the loan ourselves, and/or we get a loan from the bank or credit union – buying shares in a company we would have collateral. We could do a bond issue.

Then we let the company work its magic - assuming it is making a profit, we can use the profits to pay off the loan. As long as the returns are higher than the interest on the loan, the foundation will gradually pay off the loan. At that point, it can use its profits to buy more shares of the company.

Share by share it could grow and grow, until it took over 51% ownership. I don't know exactly what would happen at that point – the other 49% of owners probably wouldn't be too happy if you just turned it into a non-profit that didn't pay dividends anymore. Maybe once it got up to 30-40% the for-profit people would be organizing poison pill defences, the price might drop because of the threat the company would stop paying out profits…

Well, it could just be structured so that the foundation-owned shares paid out to charities, while the privately owned paid out profits like normal. Crossing the 51% line wouldn't even have to mean a lot. The one thing is that the foundation would have control of the company at that point - could be the for-profit people might not like the innovative new directions the company was going in.

There is also a thing happening these days on the stock market, where successful companies don't actually pay out profits anymore. But that's often because they are plowing the profits back into the company to make them grow, so the company goes up in value.

Paying out dividends and having your stock go up in value do work out to be pretty similar things. So with loans you could probably do the same thing, buying stock, selling it to pay off the loan, then getting a new loan to buy more stock, three steps forward, two steps back.

These strategies are a risk for whoever is making the loans, and I can't promise it would happen particularly quickly. More effective company-buying strategies would probably involve some sacrifices on our part, even if it's just lower returns. But the above is a way of turning a company into a non-profit, pretty much just out of nothing. If a foundation owns 1% of a company, it can use it's 1% of the profits to buy 2% of the company.

I hope I'm not giving anybody nightmares. Before you get too excited, I should note that – depending on where you live – there could be legal barriers that prevent you from doing that.

It would probably be illegal in the USA, for example. Which is actually really funny, because they did recently change the laws to allow non-profit charitable foundations to own companies.

From 1969 to 2018 foundations could only own a maximum of 20% of a business in the USA. There were good reasons why it was illegal, people had really been using it to avoid taxes. But it did close off a whole type of companies from existing.

But the Philanthropic Enterprise Act in the Bipartisan Budget Act of 2018 made foundation ownership legal. Foundations can now own 100% of a business, as long as they meet certain criteria. These include board independence, and that they *do* donate all their profits to charity.

So all good up to there. But then there's a passage that says foundations can only own companies if *"all the private foundation's ownership interests in the business enterprise were acquired by means other than by purchase."*

I'm not a lawyer, but it seems reasonably clear to me that foundations are only allowed to own a company if they didn't buy the shares. It's like they are putting in special clauses just to keep people from doing anything cool.

That's just the USA - in Canada, for example, private foundations have a similar maximum ownership %, but the rules are less strict for public foundations. BUT there's another law in another book - in both Canada and the USA - where foundations have to donate a % of their holdings to charity every year.

In the US it's 5%, Canada 3.5% - so if a foundation in the US has an endowment of $10 million, it has to donate half a million every year. That would really cut into the self-buying funds, and prevent the running of an at-cost foundation owned business.

That's all just foundations - I imagine there would be other ways to have a self-buying company. It could just be a cooperative, for example. My point here is more just that you never know what is going to blindside you.

I'd like to be able to tell you what ownership structures would work for non-profit businesses in your jurisdiction. But there's a lack of information about that, and it really goes beyond the scope of this article. Every country is going to be different. So I can't really do much more than provide a few anecdotes.

As a general rule of thumb, though, one of the safest strategies is just stick to whatever other people are doing. If someone is running a business as an investor-owned cooperative where mutual funds own a company that invests in mutual funds (like the Vanguard group), then that probably means that is legal where you are. They've done all the legal research themselves, and nobody's stopped them.

Even that isn't 100% foolproof though. For example Newman's Own was actually operating in contravention of US foundation law for quite a while. This world eh? The foundation owned 100% of the company, when 20% was the maximum.

They got a five-year exemption after Paul Newman's death, then another five. But as of 2018 they were facing an impossibly high punitive tax bill – 200% of the value of the company beyond the permitted 20% ownership stake. That would have obviously forced them to sell the company, but they are good now with the new rules - they were actually one of the main actors lobbying for the 2018 change in the tax code.

So while you can't have self-buying foundations in the US, you can donate your shares to a foundation. Hopefully now that it is legal we will see more of that. It's a tough strategy for us little guys, but if huge numbers did start donating a few shares each we could eventually foundationalize some big companies.

It might be a better strategy for you masters of industry out there. You can't run your company forever – sure, you can pass it down to those ingrates in your family, but they'll probably just screw it up, you know them. Better to donate it to a foundation that can manage your legacy, and donate a mountain to some assorted charities of your choice. Like they do in Denmark.

As I was finishing this article, the outdoor clothing company Patagonia was donated to a non-profit foundation by its founder, Yvon Chouinard. All its future profits – if not reinvested in the company – will go towards fighting climate change. Patagonia estimates that will work out to be about US $100 million per year.

Cooperative Not-of-the-State

A big advantage with all this business of creating cooperatives or turning existing businesses into non-profits is that it doesn't take anything from anybody. Aside from the loss in sales that any company costs its competition.

Maybe some of you are vengeful, but I see not-taking as a major advantage. People get really up in arms over tiny wealth taxes. We turn Amazon into a cooperative or a foundation, and Jeff Bezos and whoever all owns Amazon's stock don't lose anything.

They sell their shares, like any other time someone sells a share in a company. Then they can use that money to go invest in other things. All it really means in this context is that there's one less avenue to getting rich.

All the people who want to be rich would have to crowd around all the other investments. So it's sort of like musical chairs. We'll cooperativize half the economy and there'll be no easy way to get really filthy rich anymore, investment funds will have to plow their money into junk bonds just to try for a decent return.

It also allows for gradual economic change. Buying Amazon would probably take a while, for one. We can slowly expand the number of cooperatives out there, company by company, learning as we go. If I was king of the world and I could snap my fingers and magically turn everything into cooperatives, I don't know if I would do it.

This is again the thing about businesses. They can just fail, even if they are awesome progressive decentralized cooperatives. Stocks go down in value, markets tank, raw materials jump in price, new competitors appear. 60% of restaurants fail in the first three years. Every company in existence today could have instead been a failed company, and they can all go broke at any time if they don't keep up.

Rapid, radical change can be a dangerous thing. What modern capitalism tends to do is concentrate the ownership of capital into the hands of people who are good at investing. That's a functional system, it keeps the lights on.

There's an important line of reasoning, that our current system is terrible but it's the best we've got. Churchill, right? If it ain't all-that-broke, don't fix it.

With any change there is always the risk things end up for the worse, it's always easy to criticize from the sidelines.

I appreciate that logic, I think a lot of us do. But at the same time the economy's a colossal s-show, isn't it? Do we really want to go on forever with our jury-rigged casino capitalism, persevering through its flailing fragility of wild carnivalesque swings, bunkering down as it eats everything in its path, while the fortunes of nations are decided by second guessers second guessing second guessers, all determining what we can buy and where we have the option to work?

There's one thing that unites us all - rich and poor, left and right, young and old, north and south - we all like to complain about the economy. What is even the long-term argument for the status-quo? We just keep chugging along, bailing water out of the ship as we go, reclaiming the oceans into land with all the junk we produce until we invent ourselves into hyper-space capitalism, where the poor have mansions on private islands and the rich have their own pleasure planets?

If we don't want to go on like this forever, there are only so many different economic models we can use. I suppose the other one that's been hovering (hovering?) in the background of this article is state ownership. Having the government own and run the economy. And that does in fact resolve a lot of the issues I have been raising in this article.

A government owned business isn't going to be motivated by profits any more than a consumer owned business, for example. Which, again, isn't to say they aren't motivated by profits, but that it's much less than with your standard capitalistic enterprise. If a government-owned business does make a profit, it just goes into the state's pockets. It could again just translate into lower prices, as well.

As long as your government purports to be a representative of the people, when the government makes money, that's you making money. Technically, we all own everything that our governments own. But in reality, the government owns it.

A big question with state-owned enterprise is to what extent they operate under market mechanisms. If they don't really have to fight to survive - perhaps because they get taxpayer subsidized handouts, or because they don't have any competition - there's plenty of economists who will warn you about how they can become bloated and inefficient.

Another question is to what extent they are independent of the politicians and bureaucrats in power. Hypothetically I suppose we could have 10 state-owned clothing companies which are all independently managed and in competition with each other.

These days we often have state-owned businesses for 'natural monopolies' - situations where it's hard to have competition. When that's the case, we've repeatedly decided it's better just to have the government run things.

Water utilities are often public, for example. If you had three taps in your sink, and you could choose which one you wanted to use, then great, there would be competition, you could pay extra for water imported from Tahiti if you wanted. But otherwise there aren't necessarily a lot of downsides to having the government run something instead of the private sector.

State-owned businesses are reasonably common around the world - even a free market stalwart like the USA has a decent amount. Everything from the mail to energy, lottery commissions, ferry services, railways.

The Scandinavian countries for example are famous for big government. Although it's worth noting that even in Norway - the OECD country with the most state ownership - only about 10% of non-agricultural employees (that was the first statistic I found) work for state-owned enterprises. So the Nordic model is a combination of state ownership with a strong vibrant market. They have a lot of cooperatives.

Having the government own most, all, or even just a lot of the economy is another story, however. The government is just always going to be powerful anyways, I don't know if we want them in charge of where you shop as well. Where do you go if the government goes bad?

Throughout history there's been a correlation between strong centralized governments and repressive regimes. And it's gotten really, really bad, sometimes. If you had to place our current societies on a line between the worst it's been in the past 100 years and utopia, we'd be fairly far to the one side.

There's always going to be bullies who want to run things - if you have a centralized power structure that's just all the easier for them. Maybe you have a great band of ethical revolutionaries that take over and work for the common good, but then one gets blackmailed with a compromising video, another gets pressured a little then sells out, the one guy who stays clean starts having loved ones die in a series of increasingly bizarre traffic accidents...

Everything else aside, humanity has just had bad experiences with radical change and a lot of the ideologies in play. I think a lot of the population is happy chug-chugging away with things as they are, we're all a little risk-adverse, there isn't the appetite. So anyone advocating for radical change is running the risk of not achieving much aside from providing a handy bogeyman for the conservatives. Or ya, things going bad and just ultimately achieving fascism variant C.

There is debate to what extent the Communism and Socialism we have seen historically was just dictators liking the ideology. The Nazis – National Socialists – were the ones fighting the socialists, a little weird that far left and far right can both be socialism. Maybe it would have been socialism for everyday poor white Germans after the final victory, but I doubt even they would have fared too well. Some centralized regimes might argue they need a strong government to resist imperialist aggressions.

Socialism shouldn't have anything to do with totalitarianism and death camps. It isn't actually about social programs like welfare handouts to the poor either, if that does naturally go along with a lot of socialist ideas. Oxford languages defines socialism as:

> *'a political and economic theory of social organization which advocates that the means of production, distribution, and exchange should be owned or regulated by the community as a whole.'*

So it's just about having the general population own and run the economy. You can actually do a lot of the stuff someone like Marx was talking about within the free market. One of his big things was having the workers own the means of production, and you can do that in capitalism, it's a worker owned cooperative.

All this about having cooperatively owned businesses is in fact a type of socialism. Arguably it's one of the only ways you can have socialism, if you don't trust the government to run the whole economy. Although, I should actually note that foundation-owned businesses aren't technically socialism - so if you like the idea but don't want to be a socialist then there's an option for you.

I wouldn't worry too much anyways, this is a distinct political agenda. A lot of people define socialism by its lack of free markets, after all. You could call it 'market socialism', although that does often get used for countries with a big government combined with straight up capitalism.

Historically there has been a lot of overlap between the cooperative movement and socialist movements. But they have been in conflict a decent amount as well - there have even been times when Socialist and Social Democratic parties have been anti-cooperative. The Christian cooperative movement has often separated itself from more socialist elements.

Political and religious neutrality has been an important issue for many in the cooperative movement over history - it's even one of the 'Rochdale Principles'. But overall I think they generally fit pretty well into the Social Democrat agenda. A more fitting term might be 'Liberal Socialism'? I don't know who came up with that, it's like they were trying to find the worst words in the English language, then combine them..

Funnily enough, you could probably call this stuff 'Conservative Socialism' as well. A lot of modern Conservatism is actually rooted in 'Liberal' ideas, so the two words can be used interchangeably sometimes. Technically a lot of modern centre-right Conservatives are Liberals complaining about the other Liberals.

Language morphs in confusing and contradictory ways sometimes - California isn't the south, Italians aren't Latinos, Greece is neither Balkan nor Eastern Europe – it's Greece. 'Liberal' is a heavily political word that has been used in a lot of different contexts by a lot of different people over long periods of time. As is Socialism, for that matter.

'Neo-Liberalism' is basically Conservativism, for example. In British Columbia where I'm from, the 'Liberal Party' was the conservative party, although they are now apparently changing their name. The joke was we're such hippies in BC that our Conservatives are Liberals, but I think really they were just trying to skim a few % of votes from people who thought they were associated with the Federal Liberal party of Justin Trudeau fame (how was that going for you?). Liberty is just another word for freedom, philosophically the NRA is a pretty 'liberal' organization. Small government socialism is very much a thing, and this is how you do it.

The point I'm going towards with all this is that there are only a limited number of working models out there. There are just ever only so many different ways of doing things. If you need to go from LA to New York, but you've decided you neither want to fly nor drive, there are alternatives, but if you don't like any of those, the options start dropping off really fast.

If we don't want a small number of rich people owning and running things, and we don't want the government doing it either, how else are we going to organize the economy, if not through stuff like cooperatives and foundations? Maybe it all sounds a little pie-in-the-sky, or comes with terrible risks-of-its-own like nobody getting rich. But we don't have an unlimited choice of infinite different ways of doing things.

Have I missed any models? The church can own things, or there's the caste system, for that matter. Those don't necessarily get around the original problems though. Feudalism? Maybe we could program an AI to run the economy, or try and just organize things by spontaneous action. Just increasing the number of small businesses is something.

Maybe there's a case for decentralized organizations like cooperatives or foundations, but without the market? Problem is there's a lot of material stuff to organize, like who gets access to what land, how much oil people get, everything.

Gotta assume everyone is going to want more, more, more. Markets are a way of getting around the need to have a central authority that makes those decisions. With markets, who gets what is determined by who has money to buy, how much they want it, who is willing to sell, and for how much.

Cooperatives are very similar to existing businesses. And from some angles that is a really big advantage. This world is a big complicated place, with lots of potential for unexpected consequences, systemic failures, counter-intuitive paradoxical effects, you name it.

Whatever your perspective, there is just always going to be a case for the economic status quo. So for me that makes a pretty strong case for organizational structures which deal with some of the problems of the existing economic order without needing any radical change.

As a model, cooperatives are in many ways a combination of two of the most common working models in our present-day society – capitalistic firms and charitable organizations. With a mixture of the advantages and disadvantages of each.

Cooperatives, businesses, charities, they all tend to have similar structures. There's a lot of organizational socio-economic entities out there with boards of directors who hire CEOs, and some pool/group of people choosing that board. Government and government owned companies can be similar as well - that kind of structure is by no means 100% of the economy, but it's fairly common.

I do worry about having these big hundred-million dollar economic entities that are just sort of drifting aimlessly through the economy. A business is a huge infinitely-complicated economic entity that means a lot of different things to a lot of different people. To their suppliers, they are a customer, to their customers a supplier, they are where people get their income, they are the competition that is costing another company sales.

Huge amounts of money flow through businesses, corruption, embezzlement are constant threats for any economic entity. Private companies are watched over by profit-hungry investors. And there's gotta be a decent amount of people watching the charities they are donating to – that's their favorite cause, they are giving people money. But the place where you buy shoes?

Boards of directors can get 'entrenched' and it's always the same people running the company. If the directors get all their buddies cushy jobs and the company goes all inefficient, that's a variation on embezzlement. Companies can just get taken over and dedicated to people's pet causes.

But those risks sound pretty manageable in the grand scheme of things. What's on the balance is that cooperatives are a way of actually having the people own and run things. "The People" being another one of those words that has been used in a lot of different contexts and taken on a lot of different meanings. But the basic underlying logic is a pretty nice thing, we us everybody.

Historically having the people run things is the exception. And it is kind of a funny concept - we'll probably still need hierarchy, bosses that run things and newcomers starting out in the mail room. It's hard for the millions of customers of a business to vote on day-to-day things like hiring decisions, whether or not to paint the factory walls, exactly how much raw materials to buy.

So there is a question of what it actually means to have 'the people' in control. The people *does* include everyone from green-haired social justice warriors to Trump supporters. But there are shared interests among us all, and with democracy we all get our individual vote - with a little luck the best candidates will does in fact get selected.

At root, I think it works out to be about companies that truly work for our interests, and operate under a different value system. It's about nobody extracting a profit, and those benefits just going to us instead.

Git 'er Done, Libbards

We know cooperatives are a working model. There's been enough of them throughout history that have been successful - depending on where you put the start point, the movement is going on 200+ years.

Credit Unions - an area where cooperatives have been particularly successful in recent years - manage just over 2 trillion in assets in the USA. That's a lot of money. But the single largest bank in America, JP Morgan Chase, has total assets worth 3.67 trillion. So that's operating on a totally different scale.

The United Nations Department for Economic and Social Affairs, with support from Rabobank, conducted a 'Global Census on Cooperatives' in 2013-14. They found that:

> *"Combined the global cooperative economy is larger than France's economy and places right behind Germany's economy as the 5th largest economic unit if it were a united country. At a national level the cooperative economy comprises over 10% of the Gross Domestic Product in 4 countries in the world (New Zealand (20%), Netherlands (18%), France (18%) and Finland (14%))"*

So again maybe it's a question of perspective. But compared to having a 'cooperative commonwealth' they are still overall a pretty fringe thing in the world economy. A study by the University of Wisconsin Center for Cooperatives found that cooperatives only make up 1% of US GDP, for example. So from this perspective of wanting to cooperativize most of the economy, the question becomes how *do* we scale up?

I don't want to generalize – and I might be going a little out on a limb – but I have a sensation that overall people in the cooperative movement tend towards idealism over realism. So when I'm looking for reason why the movement hasn't reached it's potential, I have to wonder if that might have something to do with it.

Maybe we need some more of that good ol' free market capitalism attitude. If we want to compete with masters of industry, we need to all collectively think and act like a master of industry. Again, capitalism has done well as a system – one of its single greatest flaws is that it's been too successful and we're destroying the world.

The big worker-owned cooperative Mondragon does this really cool thing where they limit executive salaries so that the highest paid employees can only make a few times that of the lowest paid. The exact ratio varies across divisions - from 3:1 to 9:1 - but the average is 5:1. So if the lowest paid workers are getting 50,000 euros a year, the CEO can't make more than 250,000.

That's really great, if we can make that work. But it is going against the laws of economics to pay a CEO $250,000 when their peers are getting millions plus stock options. Someone *can* be worth $10 million, because of their human capital - there's only so many people with 30 year's proven history running billion dollar corporations, who know all the tricks of the industry, with friends in all the right places.

The compensation a director gets is the cost of an input, just like the electricity, wood, or chemicals in a manufacturing plant. That is something fundamentally different from making a million dollars a year because you own a factory that someone else is running. If top CEOs are making $10 million that's probably because that's what it takes to get them to come work somewhere, and if you pay $8 million you get someone else.

One of the things MEC did was limit total compensation, while requiring that the directors had huge amounts of experience running giant mega-corporations. So they limited their pool of potential directors to a small group of compensation-conscious people, while paying them a fraction of what they could make elsewhere.

Maybe we should hire one of the top corporate raiders, and pay them the total of what they would get running a Fortune 500 company. Then tell them, OK YOU WORK FOR US NOW! Now us customers are the 'shareholders' you're so obsessed about. We'd just have to deprogram them first, maybe we take them backpacking across Asia for a couple months or something.

I mean, I don't really know, these are just suggestions. A bit of devil's advocate, even. But maybe these are the kinds of things we should be thinking about. I'm definitely not criticizing Mondragon, more just saying that we shouldn't necessarily be so optimistic that we'll always be able to get stuff like that to work.

Executive pay does get truly ridiculous sometimes, and it can go beyond market forces if the directors are just voting themselves pay raises. You *do* get a different type of person if you pay more, but that cuts both ways. So maybe it's about finding some sort of middle ground - there's worse things than letting the young people dream about becoming millionaire cooperative CEOs.

Likewise we could try and maintain the incentive structures of modern capitalism. As venture capitalists know, a lot of businesses fail, but the ones that succeed make a lot of money. U.S. Bureau of Labor Statistics data shows that 20% of new businesses fail in the first two years of being open, 45% fail in the first five years, and only 25% are still going after 15 years.

Are we in the cooperative movement so magically awesome that we can beat those numbers? If so, by how much? Maybe we don't need to feel guilty if a successful cooperative pays out 10, 20, 50 times the original investment. Maybe that's what it takes to make it worth our while. The big important thing is creating a business that lasts the test of time, it's not a big deal if it's paying out investors for 20 years if the company survives 100+ years as a nonprofit.

We don't need to start out giving a % of the profits to charities either. People starting cooperatives do that sometimes, do they? That's an honorable thing to do, but it is going to directly mean higher prices. Maybe better focusing on getting established and having the lowest prices possible. Then in ten years when we have created a successful company we can start gouging people for puppy rescue and feeding the children.

Just in general I think we've got lots of room to up our game. MEC had $462 million in sales in 2018. The owners of a company like that shouldn't be scrambling to raise $50,000 on GoFundMe when there's a surprise announcement that the board of directors is selling the company.

Would it have been that hard for MEC to squirrel away a few million over the years for a legal defence fund? It's not like we're some media mogul that can just sell off their tabloid division when they need some emergency cash.

MEC was having financial troubles for a long time before the bankruptcy was announced. So maybe more of us customer-owners should have taken it on ourselves to research what exactly was going on. If we did need to raise funds to bail the company out, we could have started on it months or even years before it became a serious issue. We could have foreseen the negative effects the coronavirus might have had from its outset.

Or if we don't think it's feasible for us to do that level of constant monitoring, then we should set up systems to do it for us. Maybe it makes sense to invest a lot in external auditing. A company that spends $500 million a year can spend an extra million on being audited every year, they could spend $5 million. Accept that it's a big cost - every company is always at risk of corruption, but decentralized cooperatives even more so. So maybe it does make sense to have a whole other set of eyes on the day-to-day management of the company.

We could hire a top notch auditing firm, some management consultants to help them, another auditing firm to audit the first auditing firm. Give them some real powers - the ability to email every member with a red flag notice, or require directors to take a lie-detector test, they could have access to a certain amount of no-questions-asked money for private detectives. That doesn't mean we don't trust our directors, we just want to be ever-vigilant, protect ourself from one in fifty-year events.

I've been going on and on about this, but finding a half-way decent set of directors isn't an intractable problem. It's done all the time by companies and charities all around the world on the regular basis. The question is just hiring a board that is as good as any other board out there, and getting them keep performing as well as any other board would.

There are exceptions, but if you pay good money to run your company, you can generally find someone who is going to do a good job. And they do also generally do what you tell them to - if you tell them to maximize profits, they'll do that. If you just tell them to break even making the best products possible, then that's what they will do.

We as a group of customers should be able to get together and vote in a good board of directors. It's worked for a lot of cooperatives in the past, and while I see challenges I think they are resolvable. If we do it properly it is probably the single best way to choose a board.

Maybe there are some arguments for trying different models. Above I was talking about using a 'customer's assembly' of say 200 randomly chosen customers to recommend candidates. Instead of just recommending candidates, that assembly could even just directly choose the board.

Maybe we could think even further outside the box. How about doing a reality TV show? Or a set of 10 riddles, and whoever answers first is on the board. Not sure how you choose the riddles, maybe that's getting too extravagant. Going the other direction, how about we just contract a recruiting company to hire us a board?

Again, it's hard to say how much of that is legal. It will again depend on your local legal framework. Companies are big regulated legal entities, so there are a lot of controls. In Canada there's a lot of regulations towards keeping boards democratic. I wouldn't even bother with the riddles strategy, honestly.

Denmark's Carlsberg brewery - the internet is telling me it's either the 3rd or 4th biggest brewery in the world - is controlled by a foundation. And what they do is have the Royal Danish Academy of Sciences and Letters elect five of its Danish members to be directors. So the board is selected from a group of about 250 prominent Danish scientists in the humanities and natural sciences.

They've been doing that since 1876, so it must be working. If you are looking for an investment, by the way, they do actually trade on NASDAQ Copenhagen. The Foundation only owns 30% of the company, but has 76% of the voting shares. The rest of the shares pay out profits to its owners, while the foundation uses its profits to fund scientific research (including some brewing-related stuff) and social initiatives through the Tuborg Foundation. In 2022 they approved a total of about US $85 million in research funding alone.

I don't know if that structure would be legal in a country like Canada. But Carlsberg just recently bought the Canadian brewery Waterloo Brewing. And I'm sure they did their due diligence, and everything in that deal was legal. So if we did want to elect our directors the same way as Carlsberg, we could move to Copenhagen and buy a shell Canadian holding company. Think outside the box people!

The Invisible Hand.. Beckons??

In the end, I can't promise you that a cooperative or foundation will be successful. Starting a cooperative is about us taking the risk. If it succeeds, we get the benefits, if it fails, we lose our investment.

If everyone is just chipping in $20 each, that isn't much to lose. But if we invest $50 million in a cooperative theme park that goes belly-up, that's a $50 million theme park that might have existed if it had been some rich guy starting it.

Likewise I've been talking about lower prices, but those aren't guaranteed either. I've definitely shopped at overpriced cooperatives before. What I'm talking about is the underlying economics of cooperatives, and in economic theory the real world can be a special case.

Maybe a lack of strong owner supervision does mean they are just a little less efficient. If we aren't tough on the staff, they might manage to get higher wages than the competition pays, driving up prices. Maybe we can't bring ourselves to do the unethical things the market demands. As it stands the global middle class has a lot of slaves working for us - there's even an online calculator if you are curious how many. Prices could go up if we cut slavery from the production process.

Not having to pay out profits does give cooperatives a fundamental advantage though. So we can mess it up a little bit and still survive in a competitive market. If that's the case, then maybe the worst is that we trade our capitalist enterprises for shiny consumer cooperatives where things cost the same amount, but there's less pollution and the workers make a little more.

That's not the biggest waste of effort, is it? The more cooperatives there are out there, the more likely it is you are going to work for one. And they tend to be nice places to work, especially if the workers do manage to get higher wages.

If nothing else we could even just have unethical cooperatives. Pretty sad state of world affairs if it's come to that. They don't necessarily have to be 'unethical', maybe just less ethical. Forget I even said unethical, just companies that keep up with the morals of the existing market, how about that? Any existing business could basically operate the exact same way as it does now, and just have lower prices if it was owned by its customers.

And, actually, there is one more option. I'm almost loath to mention it - it's a little heretical, I'll be nervous next time there's a thunderstorm, believe you me. But an inherent truth of the marketplace is that any business can survive, as long as people are buying its products.

That isn't saying anything profound or contentious there, really I'm just saying that successful businesses do generally tend to be successful. There's probably a few situations where that isn't the case, but they are outliers, if you find one, betcha I'll call it an exception that proves the rule.

So – technically, at least – a cooperative can survive even if it doesn't have the lowest priced products on the market. It just needs enough people who don't care and keep shopping there anyways.

So if for whatever reason we do like a particular cooperative - anything from nostalgia for a business we created, to preferring the non-profit model, or the retail outlet having a good location down the road, not wanting to use slave labour - then we can keep it afloat if we are willing to make the sacrifice of paying more. Anyways, ignore me, best we at least match market prices, right?

One way or another, if we want cooperatives I think we should assume we will have to create them ourselves. The all-mighty vaguely defined *they* don't seem particularly motivated to create them for us. Although like I was talking about above, there are models where investors can get rich creating cooperatives.

If a cooperative movement can gain a reputation as creating successful businesses, and can offer better-than-market returns for a given level of risk, money can be expect to flow there. Perhaps investors would be better off just privately owning any company that ends up being successful, but loans are a thing, lots of people do make lots of money just lending money out.

Me personally, I don't feel like I'm in the right place to do any of the spearheading sort of work involved in starting a cooperative, at least not in the immediate future. Maybe talk to me in a few years.

My work background isn't actually in cooperatives, but running my own small business. Probably freelance consultant is more accurate, actually - research, writing, translations, stuff like that. But I'm more than willing to put in some real volunteer hours, if somebody comes up with something that grabs me. I can do any number of things, and you can put me down for 10k flyers delivered to people's doors.

Shouldn't there be a Kickstarter type site specifically for cooperatives by now? I'm sure there's some little things, but I don't see any big famous websites. It would be pretty cool to see a bunch of cooperatives you could invest in, maybe with a regional database of existing cooperatives you could join. I guess it doesn't exist because nobody started it, myself included.

Beyond anything like that, there is actually a quick and easy way we can all support cooperatives - just by shopping at the cooperatives that exist right now. There are lots of them out there – maybe they don't always stand out so much, but if you look you should be able to find some. Personally I do like to support the movement whenever I can, so I try to go to a cooperative even if X-mart has the same product for 10% less.

Otherwise, what kind of economy do we really expect to have, running things on greed? Greed does work some wonders, but it is also one of the seven deadlies. The existence of every problem is a boon for those who are paid to fix it. While problems with a product become terrible secrets to be hidden at all costs.

The profit motive does naturally lead to over-consumption, and over-consumption is something we are really having trouble with right now. A lot of for-profit companies are only happy if their sales are growing 5-10%+ a year, while a cooperative could lower its sales by 10-20% if that's what it took to make longer lasting products or save the world.

So many of our economic decisions end up being made by various types of fund managers, who are all fighting for their economic lives to stay as far ahead of the market as they can. Can we really expect them to behave differently than they do? The money just goes to someone else anyways, if they don't get that extra point of returns.

Greed isn't going to go away. But different systems deal with human nature and the implications of the human condition in different ways. The fact that consumer owned cooperatives do ultimately answer to the customer themselves does create real mechanisms by which they do what the consumer wants. This is a real way to run companies on a different set of values.

Depending on how you look at it, this isn't really anything radical. But maybe we don't need radical. We can make the world a better place just by making things a little cheaper and more durable. Getting a raise and having things cost less are actually fairly equivalent. A large part of why the rich get and stay rich is through 5-10% profit margins.

The economy is where we live, work, it washes our cars, cuts our hair, even walks our dogs. It provides us with comfort food when we are down, carries us around the world and gives us a place to stay when we want adventure. Good luck achieving much of anything without using the economy. Given its profound importance to our day-to-day life it would be nice if we everyone were a little bit more in control of it. Or at least not so much at its mercy.

We can create our own economy from within the existing economy. It's called the free market because it's free - we're free to make what we want of it. We can just sidestep the whole materialistic casino rat race, let them do their thing, we'll do our own. We can bring the economy down to earth, if cooperatives provide you with all the things you need, then you don't have to be a part of the machine.

Given the socio-economic-environmental death spiral we as a planet are hurtling down, there's a fairly solid argument that finding better ways of doing things is in fact a life-or-death question. We humans have built pyramids, walked on the moon. Getting a few non-profit businesses off the ground should be easy in comparison.

Thank you for reading! These articles and other are available for free at my website, www.dylankyle.com.

If you enjoyed reading them, please follow me on social media! I must be five kinds of blacklisted, so you probably won't hear about me otherwise.

I also accept donations — the idea is to put this stuff out there for free without any kinds of advertising. In writing this article I received no compensation in any form from any bands, companies, anybody.

You can sign up for my mailing list at mail@dylankyle.com

Manufactured by Amazon.ca
Bolton, ON